THE YALE SHAKESPEARE

Edited by

Wilbur L. Cross   Tucker Brooke

Published under the Direction
of the
Department of English, Yale University,
on the Fund
Given to the Yale University Press in 1917
by the Members of the
Kingsley Trust Association
(Scroll and Key Society of Yale College)
to Commemorate the Seventy-Fifth Anniversary
of the Founding of the Society

·: *The Yale Shakespeare* :·

LOVE'S LABOUR'S LOST

EDITED BY

WILBUR L. CROSS

AND

TUCKER BROOKE

NEW HAVEN · YALE UNIVERSITY PRESS
LONDON · GEOFFREY CUMBERLEGE
OXFORD UNIVERSITY PRESS

TABLE OF CONTENTS

The facsimile opposite reproduces the frontispiece to 'Love's Labour's Lost' in Rowe's edition of Shakespeare (1709). The scene depicted is the visit of the pretended Muscovites near the opening of V. ii.

[DRAMATIS PERSONÆ.

FERDINAND, *King of Navarre*

BEROWNE,
LONGAVILLE, } *three Lords attending upon the King in his retirement*
DUMAINE,

BOYET, } *Lords attending upon the Princess of France*
MARCADE,

DON ADRIANO DE ARMADO, *a fantastical Spaniard*

NATHANIEL, *a Curate*

DULL, *a Constable*

HOLOFERNES, *a Schoolmaster*

COSTARD, *a Clown*

MOTH, *Page to Don Adriano de Armado*

A Forester

PRINCESS OF FRANCE

ROSALINE,
MARIA, } *Ladies attending on the Princess*
KATHARINE,

JAQUENETTA, *a country Wench*

Officers and Other Attendants upon the King and Princess

SCENE: *Navarre*]

Dramatis Personæ; *cf. n.*

Love's Labour's Lost

ACT FIRST

Scene One

[The King of Navarre's Park]

*Enter Ferdinand King of Navarre, Berowne,
Longaville, and Dumaine.*

King. Let fame, that all hunt after in their lives,
Live register'd upon our brazen tombs,
And then grace us in the disgrace of death;
When, spite of cormorant devouring Time,   **4**
Th' endeavour of this present breath may buy
That honour which shall bate his scythe's keen edge,
And make us heirs of all eternity.
Therefore, brave conquerors,—for so you are,   **8**
That war against your own affections
And the huge army of the world's desires,—
Our late edict shall strongly stand in force:
Navarre shall be the wonder of the world;   **12**
Our court shall be a little academe,
Still and contemplative in living art.
You three, Berowne, Dumaine, and Longaville,
Have sworn for three years' term to live with me, **16**
My fellow-scholars, and to keep those statutes
That are recorded in this schedule here:
Your oaths are pass'd; and now subscribe your names,
That his own hand may strike his honour down   **20**
That violates the smallest branch herein.

Love's Labour's Lost; *cf. n.*   4 cormorant: *ravenous*
6 bate: *blunt*   12 Navarre; *cf. n.*   13 academe: *academy*
14 living art: *the art of living; cf. n.*   19 subscribe: *sign*

If you are arm'd to do, as sworn to do,
Subscribe to your deep oaths, and keep it too.

    Long. I am resolv'd; 'tis but a three years' fast: 24
The mind shall banquet, though the body pine:
Fat paunches have lean pates, and dainty bits
Make rich the ribs, but bankrupt quite the wits.

    Dum. My loving lord, Dumaine is mortified: 28
The grosser manner of these world's delights
He throws upon the gross world's baser slaves:
To love, to wealth, to pomp, I pine and die;
With all these living in philosophy.   32

    Ber. I can but say their protestation over;
So much, dear liege, I have already sworn,
That is, to live and study here three years.
But there are other strict observances;   36
As, not to see a woman in that term,
Which I hope well is not enrolled there:
And one day in a week to touch no food,
And but one meal on every day beside;   40
The which I hope is not enrolled there:
And then, to sleep but three hours in the night,
And not be seen to wink of all the day,—
When I was wont to think no harm all night   44
And make a dark night too of half the day,—
Which I hope well is not enrolled there.
O! these are barren tasks, too hard to keep,
Not to see ladies, study, fast, not sleep.   48

    King. Your oath is pass'd to pass away from these.

    Ber. Let me say no, my liege, an if you please.
I only swore to study with your Grace,

22 arm'd: *ready*   26 pates: *heads*
27 wits: *faculties of the mind*
28 mortified: *dead so far as pleasures and passions are concerned*
32 all these: *i.e. love, wealth, pomp*   38 there: *i.e. in the schedule*
43 wink of: *close the eyes during*
47 barren: *fruitless, futile*   50 an if: *if*

And stay here in your court for three years' space. 52
   Long. You swore to that, Berowne, and to the rest.
   Ber. By yea and nay, sir, then I swore in jest.
What is the end of study? let me know.
   King. Why, that to know which else we should not
     know. 56
   Ber. Things hid and barr'd, you mean, from com-
     mon sense?
   King. Ay, that is study's godlike recompense.
   Ber. Come on then; I will swear to study so,
To know the thing I am forbid to know; 60
As thus: to study where I well may dine,
   When I to feast expressly am forbid;
Or study where to meet some mistress fine,
   When mistresses from common sense are hid; 64
Or, having sworn too hard-a-keeping oath,
Study to break it, and not break my troth.
If study's gain be thus, and this be so,
Study knows that which yet it doth not know. 68
Swear me to this, and I will ne'er say no.
   King. These be the stops that hinder study quite,
And train our intellects to vain delight.
   Ber. Why, all delights are vain; but that most
     vain 72
Which, with pain purchas'd, doth inherit pain:
As, painfully to pore upon a book,
   To seek the light of truth; while truth the while
Doth falsely blind the eyesight of his look: 76
   Light seeking light doth light of light beguile:
So, ere you find where light in darkness lies,
Your light grows dark by losing of your eyes.

54 By yea and nay: *i.e. by the most positive oath of affirmation **and**
  denial   57 common sense: *ordinary sight or perception*
62 feast; *cf. n.*   67, 68 *Cf. n.*   73 *Cf. n.*
76 his: *its*   77 beguile: *deprive*   79 light: *i.e. sight*

Study me how to please the eye indeed,   80
    By fixing it upon a fairer eye,
Who dazzling so, that eye shall be his heed,
    And give him light that it was blinded by.
Study is like the heaven's glorious sun,   84
    That will not be deep-search'd with saucy looks:
Small have continual plodders ever won,
    Save base authority from others' books.
These earthly godfathers of heaven's lights,   88
    That give a name to every fixed star,
Have no more profit of their shining nights
    Than those that walk and wot not what they are.
Too much to know is to know nought but fame;   92
And every godfather can give a name.
    King. How well he's read, to reason against read-
        ing!
    Dum. Proceeded well, to stop all good proceeding!
    Long. He weeds the corn, and still lets grow the
        weeding.   96
    Ber. The spring is near, when green geese are a-
        breeding.
    Dum. How follows that?
    Ber.   Fit in his place and time.
    Dum. In reason nothing.
    Ber.   Something, then, in rime.
    King. Berowne is like an envious sneaping frost 100
That bites the first-born infants of the spring.
    Ber. Well, say I am: why should proud summer
        boast
    Before the birds have any cause to sing?
Why should I joy in any abortive birth?   104

80-83 Study me . . . blinded by; *cf. n.*   85 saucy: *bold*
86 Small: *little*   88-93 *Cf. n.*
91 wot: *know*   95 Proceeded; *cf. n.*
97 green geese: *grass-fed goslings, i.e. simpletons*   99 *Cf. n.*
100 sneaping: *nipping*   101 infants: *buds or flowers*

At Christmas I no more desire a rose
Than wish a snow in May's new-fangled shows;
But like of each thing that in season grows.
So you, to study now it is too late,   108
Climb o'er the house to unlock the little gate.

 King. Well, sit you out: go home, Berowne: adieu!

 Ber. No, my good lord; I have sworn to stay with
  you:
And though I have for barbarism spoke more   112
 Than for that angel knowledge you can say,
Yet confident I'll keep what I have sworn,
 And bide the penance of each three years' day.
Give me the paper; let me read the same;   116
And to the strictest decrees I'll write my name.

 King. How well this yielding rescues thee from
  shame!

 Ber. 'Item. That no woman shall come within a mile of my court.' Hath this been pro- 120
claimed?

Long. Four days ago.

 Ber. Let's see the penalty. 'On pain of losing
her tongue.' Who devised this penalty?   124

Long. Marry, that did I.

Ber.   Sweet lord, and why?

Long. To fright them hence with that dread penalty.

[*Ber.*] A dangerous law against gentility!

 'Item. If any man be seen to talk with a wo- 128
man within the term of three years, he shall
endure such public shame as the rest of the
court can possibly devise.'

---

106 new-fangled shows; *cf. n.*   109 *Cf. n.*
110 sit you out: *withdraw* 114 confident: *I am confident; cf. n.*
115 each three years' day: *each day for three years*
119 Item: *likewise*   127 gentility: *courtesy*

This article, my liege, yourself must break;   132
  For well you know here comes in embassy
The French king's daughter with yourself to speak—
  A maid of grace and complete majesty—
About surrender up of Aquitaine   136
  To her decrepit, sick, and bed-rid father.
Therefore this article is made in vain,
  Or vainly comes th' admired princess hither.
    King. What say you, lords? why, this was quite
      forgot.   140
    Ber. So study evermore is overshot:
While it doth study to have what it would,
It doth forget to do the thing it should;
And when it hath the thing it hunteth most,   144
'Tis won as towns with fire; so won, so lost.
    King. We must of force dispense with this decree;
She must lie here on mere necessity.
    Ber. Necessity will make us all forsworn   148
  Three thousand times within this three years' space:
For every man with his affects is born,
  Not by might master'd, but by special grace.
If I break faith, this word shall speak for me: 152
I am forsworn 'on mere necessity.'
So to the laws at large I write my name: [*Signs.*]
  And he that breaks them in the least degree
Stands in attainder of eternal shame.   156
    Suggestions are to others as to me;
But I believe, although I seem so loath,
I am the last that will last keep his oath.
But is there no quick recreation granted?   160
    King. Ay, that there is. Our court, you know, is
      haunted

147 lie: *lodge*   mere: *absolute*   150 affects: *affections, passions*
151 special grace: *divine help*   156 in attainder: *convicted*
157 Suggestions: *temptations*   160 quick: *lively*

With a refined traveller of Spain,
A man in all the world's new fashion planted,
   That hath a mint of phrases in his brain;   164
One who the music of his own vain tongue
   Doth ravish like enchanting harmony;
A man of complements, whom right and wrong
   Have chose as umpire of their mutiny.   168
This child of fancy, that Armado hight,
   For interim to our studies shall relate
In high-born words the worth of many a knight
   From tawny Spain lost in the world's debate.   172
How you delight, my lords, I know not, I;
But, I protest, I love to hear him lie,
And I will use him for my minstrelsy.

   Ber. Armado is a most illustrious wight,   176
A man of fire-new words, fashion's own knight.

   Long. Costard the swain and he shall be our sport;
And, so to study, three years is but short.

*Enter a Constable [Dull] with Costard
with a Letter.*

   Const. Which is the duke's own person?   180
   Ber. This, fellow. What wouldst?
   Const. I myself reprehend his own person, for
I am his Grace's tharborough: but I would see
his own person in flesh and blood.   184
   Ber. This is he.
   Const. Signior Arm—Arm—commends you.
There's villainy abroad: this letter will tell you
more.   188

165 who: *whom*   167 complements: *accomplishments*
169 hight: *is called*   171 high-born: *lofty*
172 debate: *warfare*   175 for my minstrelsy: *as my minstrel*
177 fire-new: *brand-new*   180 duke's: *i.e. king's*
182 reprehend: *i.e. represent*
183 tharborough: *third borough (constable)*

Cost. Sir, the contempts thereof are as touching me.

King. A letter from the magnificent Armado.

Ber. How low soever the matter, I hope in 192
God for high words.

Long. A high hope for a low heaven: God
grant us patience!

Ber. To hear, or forbear laughing?   196

Long. To hear meekly, sir, and ᵗo laugh
moderately, or to forbear both.

Ber. Well, sir, be it as the style shall give us
cause to climb in the merriness.   200

Cost. The matter is to me, sir, as concerning
Jaquenetta. The manner of it is, I was taken
with the manner.

Ber. In what manner?   204

Cost. In manner and form following, sir; all
those three: I was seen with her in the manor-
house, sitting with her upon the form, and taken
following her into the park; which, put together, 208
is, in manner and form following. Now, sir, for
the manner,—it is the manner of a man to speak
to a woman, for the form,—in some form.

Ber. For the following, sir?   212

Cost. As it shall follow in my correction; and
God defend the right!

King. Will you hear this letter with attention?

Ber. As we would hear an oracle.   216

Cost. Such is the simplicity of man to hearken
after the flesh.

189 contempts: *i.e. contents*
191 magnificent: *showy, vainglorious*
194 low heaven: *i.e. moderate pleasure*
203 with the manner (mainour): *in the act*
207 form: *bench*   213 correction: *punishment*

King. [*Reads.*] 'Great deputy, the welkin's vice-gerent, and sole dominator of Navarre, my soul's 220 earth's God, and body's fostering patron,—'

Cost. Not a word of Costard yet.

King. [*Reads.*] 'So it is,—'

Cost. It may be so; but if he say it is so, he 224 is, in telling true, but so.—

King. Peace!

Cost. Be to me and every man that dares not fight.   228

King. No words!

Cost. Of other men's secrets, I beseech you.

King. [*Reads.*] 'So it is, besieged with sable-coloured melancholy, I did commend the black-op- 232 pressing humour to the most wholesome physic of thy health-giving air; and, as I am a gentle-man, betook myself to walk. The time when? About the sixth hour; when beasts most graze, 236 birds best peck, and men sit down to that nourishment which is called supper: so much for the time when. Now for the ground which; which, I mean, I walked upon: it is ycleped 240 thy park. Then for the place where; where, I mean, I did encounter that most obscene and preposterous event, that draweth from my snow-white pen the ebon-coloured ink, which here thou 244 viewest, beholdest, surveyest, or seest. But to the place where, it standeth north-north-east and by east from the west corner of thy curious-knotted garden. There did I see that low-spirited 248 swain, that base minnow of thy mirth,—'

Cost. Me?

240 ycleped: *called*
247 curious-knotted: *fancifully laid out in intricate beds*

King. [*Reads.*] 'that unlettered small-knowing
soul,—'

Cost. Me?   252

King. [*Reads.*] 'that shallow vessel,—'

Cost. Still me?

King. [*Reads.*] 'which, as I remember, hight
Costard,—'   256

Cost. O me!

King. [*Reads.*] 'sorted and consorted, contrary
to thy established proclaimed edict and continent
canon, with—with,—O! with—but with this I 260
passion to say wherewith,—'

Cost. With a wench.

King. [*Reads.*] 'with a child of our grandmother
Eve, a female; or, for thy more sweet under- 264
standing, a woman.   Him I,—as my ever-
esteemed duty pricks me on,—have sent to thee,
to receive the meed of punishment, by thy sweet
Grace's officer, Anthony Dull; a man of good 268
repute, carriage, bearing, and estimation.'

Dull. Me, an 't shall please you; I am Anthony
Dull.

King. [*Reads.*] 'For Jaquenetta,—so is the
weaker vessel called which I apprehended with the 272
aforesaid swain,—I keep her as a vessel of thy law's
fury; and shall, at the least of thy sweet notice,
bring her to trial.   Thine, in all compliments of
devoted and heart-burning heat of duty,   276
               Don Adriano de Armado.'

Ber. This is not so well as I looked for, but
the best that ever I heard

258 sorted: *associated*
259 continent: *i.e. containing a summary of offenses*
261 passion: *grieve*

King. Ay, the best for the worst. But, sirrah,
what say you to this?   280

Cost. Sir, I confess the wench.

King. Did you hear the proclamation?

Cost. I do confess much of the hearing it, but
little of the marking of it.   284

King. It was proclaimed a year's imprison-
ment to be taken with a wench.

Cost. I was taken with none, sir: I was taken
with a damsel.   288

King. Well, it was proclaimed 'damsel.'

Cost. This was no damsel neither, sir: she
was a virgin.

King. It is so varied too; for it was pro-
claimed 'virgin.'   293

Cost. If it were, I deny her virginity: I was
taken with a maid.

King. This maid will not serve your turn, sir. 296

Cost. This maid will serve my turn, sir.

King. Sir, I will pronounce your sentence:
you shall fast a week with bran and water.

Cost. I had rather pray a month with mutton 300
and porridge.

King. And Don Armado shall be your keeper.
My Lord Berowne, see him deliver'd o'er:
And go we, lords, to put in practice that,   304
   Which each to other hath so strongly sworn.
        [*Exeunt King, Longaville, and Dumaine.*]
Ber. I'll lay my head to any good man's hat,
   These oaths and laws will prove an idle scorn.
Sirrah, come on.   308

Cost. I suffer for the truth, sir: for true it is

284 marking of: *paying attention to*
288 damsel: *a young unmarried woman of good birth*
300 mutton: *slang for 'loose woman'*   306 lay: *wager*

I was taken with Jaquenetta, and Jaquenetta is
a true girl; and therefore welcome the sour cup of
prosperity! Affliction may one day smile again; 312
and till then, sit thee down, sorrow! *Exeunt.*

Scene Two

[*The Same*]

Enter Armado and Moth his Page.

Arm. Boy, what sign is it when a man of
great spirit grows melancholy?

Boy. A great sign, sir, that he will look sad.

Arm. Why, sadness is one and the self-same 4
thing, dear imp.

Boy. No, no; O Lord, sir, no.

Arm. How canst thou part sadness and melancholy, my tender juvenal? 8

Boy. By a familiar demonstration of the
working, my tough senior.

Arm. Why tough senior? why tough senior?

Boy. Why tender juvenal? why tender juve- 12
nal?

Arm. I spoke it, tender juvenal, as a congruent epitheton appertaining to thy young
days, which we may nominate tender. 16

Boy. And I, tough senior, as an appertinent
title to your old time, which we may name tough.

Arm. Pretty, and apt.

Boy. How mean you, sir? I pretty, and my 20
saying apt? or I apt, and my saying pretty?

Arm. Thou pretty, because little.

5 imp: *child*   14 congruent epitheton: *suitable epithet*
16 nominate: *call*   17 appertinent: *appropriate*

Boy. Little pretty, because little. Wherefore apt?   24

Arm. And therefore apt, because quick.

Boy. Speak you this in my praise, master?

Arm. In thy condign praise.

Boy. I will praise an eel with the same 28 praise.

Arm. What! that an eel is ingenious?

Boy. That an eel is quick.

Arm. I do say thou art quick in answers: 32 thou heat'st my blood.

Boy. I am answered, sir.

Arm. I love not to be crossed.

Boy. [*Aside.*] He speaks the mere contrary: 36 crosses love not him.

Arm. I have promised to study three years with the duke.

Boy. You may do it in an hour, sir.   40

Arm. Impossible.

Boy. How many is one thrice told?

Arm. I am ill at reckoning; it fitteth the spirit of a tapster.   44

Boy. You are a gentleman and a gamester, sir.

Arm. I confess both: they are both the varnish of a complete man.   48

Boy. Then, I am sure you know how much the gross sum of deuce-ace amounts to.

Arm. It doth amount to one more than two.

Boy. Which the base vulgar do call three.   52

Arm. True.

Boy. Why, sir, is this such a piece of study? Now, here is three studied, ere ye'll thrice wink;

---

37 crosses: *coins (which had crosses on them)*

and how easy it is to put 'years' to the word 56
'three,' and study three years in two words, the
dancing horse will tell you.

Arm. A most fine figure!

Boy. To prove you a cipher.   60

Arm. I will hereupon confess I am in love;
and as it is base for a soldier to love, so am I in
love with a base wench. If drawing my sword
against the humour of affection would deliver 64
me from the reprobate thought of it, I would
take Desire prisoner, and ransom him to any
French courtier for a new devised curtsy. I
think scorn to sigh: methinks I should out- 68
swear Cupid. Comfort me, boy: what great men
have been in love?

Boy. Hercules, master.

Arm. Most sweet Hercules! More authority, 72
dear boy, name more; and, sweet my child, let
them be men of good repute and carriage.

Boy. Samson, master: he was a man of good
carriage, great carriage, for he carried the town- 76
gates on his back like a porter; and he was in love.

Arm. O well-knit Samson! strong-jointed
Samson! I do excel thee in my rapier as much as
thou didst me in carrying gates. I am in love 80
too. Who was Samson's love, my dear Moth?

Boy. A woman, master.

Arm. Of what complexion?

Boy. Of all the four, or the three, or the 84
two, or one of the four.

Arm. Tell me precisely of what complexion.

Boy. Of the sea-water green, sir.

---

58 dancing horse; *cf. n.*   59 figure: *illustration*
64 humour of affection: *caprice of being in love*
68 think: *think it*   83 complexion: *disposition; cf. n.*

Arm. Is that one of the four complexions?   88

Boy. As I have read, sir; and the best of them too.

Arm. Green indeed is the colour of lovers; but to have a love of that colour, methinks 92 Samson had small reason for it. He surely affected her for her wit.

Boy. It was so, sir, for she had a green wit.

Arm. My love is most immaculate white and 96 red.

Boy. Most maculate thoughts, master, are masked under such colours.

Arm. Define, define, well-educated infant.   100

Boy. My father's wit, and my mother's tongue, assist me!

Arm. Sweet invocation of a child; most pretty and pathetical!   104

Boy. If she be made of white and red,
     Her faults will ne'er be known,
   For blushing cheeks by faults are bred,
     And fears by pale white shown: 108
   Then if she fear, or be to blame,
     By this you shall not know,
   For still her cheeks possess the same
     Which native she doth owe.   112

A dangerous rime, master, against the reason of white and red.

Arm. Is there not a ballet, boy, of the King and the Beggar?   116

Boy. The world was very guilty of such a ballet some three ages since; but I think now

94 affected: *liked*   wit: *understanding*
95 green wit; *cf. n.*
112 native: *naturally*   owe: *own, possess*
115 ballet: *ballad*
104 pathetical: *touching*
115, 116 *Cf. n.*
118 ages: *generations*

'tis not to be found; or, if it were, it would
neither serve for the writing nor the tune.   120

Arm. I will have that subject newly writ o'er,
that I may example my digression by some
mighty precedent. Boy, I do love that country
girl that I took in the park with the rational 124
hind Costard: she deserves well.

Boy. [*Aside.*] To be whipped; and yet a
better love than my master.

Arm. Sing, boy: my spirit grows heavy in 128
love.

Boy. And that's great marvel, loving a light
wench.

Arm. I say, sing.   132

Boy. Forbear till this company be past.

Enter Clown [*Costard*], *Constable* [*Dull*],
and Wench [*Jaquenetta*].

Const. Sir, the duke's pleasure is, that you
keep Costard safe: and you must suffer him to take
no delight nor no penance, but a' must fast three 136
days a week.   For this damsel, I must keep her
at the park; she is allowed for the day-woman.
Fare you well.

Arm. I do betray myself with blushing. Maid! 140

Maid. [*Jaq.*] Man?

Arm. I will visit thee at the lodge.

Maid. That's hereby.

Arm. I know where it is situate.   144

Maid. Lord, how wise you are!

Arm. I will tell thee wonders.

Maid. With that face?

122 digression: *deviation from my nature, i.e. debasement*
124 rational: *reasoning, i.e. not stupid*   127 love: *lover*
136 a': *he*   138 allowed: *approved of*   day-woman: *dairy-woman*

Arm. I love thee.   148

Maid. So I heard you say.

Arm. And so farewell.

Maid. Fair weather after you!

Const. Come, Jaquenetta, away!   152

      Exeunt [*Dull and Jaquenetta*].

Arm. Villain, thou shalt fast for thy offences
ere thou be pardoned.

Clow. Well, sir, I hope, when I do it, I shall
do it on a full stomach.   156

Arm. Thou shalt be heavily punished.

Clow. I am more bound to you than your
fellows, for they are but lightly rewarded.

Arm. Take away this villain: shut him up.   160

Boy. Come, you transgressing slave: away!

Clow. Let me not be pent up, sir: I will fast,
being loose.

Boy. No, sir; that were fast and loose: thou 164
shalt to prison.

Clow. Well, if ever I do see the merry days of
desolation that I have seen, some shall see—

Boy. What shall some see?   168

Clow. Nay, nothing, Master Moth, but what
they look upon. It is not for prisoners to be
too silent in their words; and therefore I will
say nothing: I thank God I have as little pa- 172
tience as another man, and therefore I can be
quiet.   *Exit* [*Costard; also Moth*].

Arm. I do affect the very ground, which is
base, where her shoe, which is baser, guided by 176
her foot, which is basest, doth tread. I shall be
forsworn,—which is a great argument of false-

164 fast and loose: *cheating game of a sharper*
167 desolation; *cf. n.* 175 affect: *love* 178 argument: *proof*

hood,—if I love. And how can that be true love
which is falsely attempted? Love is a familiar; 180
Love is a devil: there is no evil angel but Love.
Yet was Samson so tempted, and he had an
excellent strength; yet was Solomon so seduced,
and he had a very good wit. Cupid's butt-shaft 184
is too hard for Hercules' club, and therefore too
much odds for a Spaniard's rapier. The first
and second cause will not serve my turn; the
passado he respects not, the duello he regards 188
not: his disgrace is to be called boy, but his
glory is to subdue men. Adieu, valour! rust,
rapier! be still, drum! for your manager is in
love; yea, he loveth. Assist me some extemporal 192
god of rime, for I am sure I shall turn sonnet.
Devise, wit; write, pen; for I am for whole
volumes in folio.   *Exit.*

180 familiar: *familiar spirit, i.e. demon*
184 butt-shaft: *arrow, without barb, for shooting at butts (targets)*
187 cause: *cause of quarrel*
188 passado: *pass, or thrust, in fencing*   duello: *duel*
191 manager: *wielder of weapons*
193 turn sonnet: *grow into a sonnet(?), turn sonneteer(?)*

ACT SECOND

Scene One

*[The King of Navarre's Park.   A Pavilion and
Tents at a distance]*

*Enter the Princess of France, with three attending
Ladies [Rosaline, Maria, Katharine,] and three
Lords [Boyet and attending Lords].*

Boyet. Now, madam, summon up your dearest
　　spirits:
Consider whom the king your father sends,
To whom he sends, and what's his embassy:
Yourself, held precious in the world's esteem,　　4
To parley with the sole inheritor
Of all perfections that a man may owe,
Matchless Navarre; the plea of no less weight
Than Aquitaine, a dowry for a queen.　　8
Be now as prodigal of all dear grace
As Nature was in making graces dear,
When she did starve the general world beside,
And prodigally gave them all to you.　　12
　　Prin. Good Lord Boyet, my beauty, though but
　　mean,
Needs not the painted flourish of your praise:
Beauty is bought by judgment of the eye,
Not utter'd by base sale of chapmen's tongues.　　16
I am less proud to hear you tell my worth
Than you much willing to be counted wise
In spending your wit in the praise of mine.
But now to task the tasker: good Boyet,　　20
You are not ignorant, all-telling fame

1 dearest: *best*　　　7 Navarre: *King of Navarre*　　plea: *suit*
16 utter'd: *sold*　　chapmen's: *shopmen's*

Doth noise abroad, Navarre hath made a vow,
Till painful study shall outwear three years,
No woman may approach his silent court: 24
Therefore to's seemeth it a needful course,
Before we enter his forbidden gates,
To know his pleasure; and in that behalf,
Bold of your worthiness, we single you   28
As our best-moving fair solicitor.
Tell him, the daughter of the King of France,
On serious business, craving quick dispatch,
Importunes personal conference with his Grace.   32
Haste, signify so much; while we attend,
Like humble-visag'd suitors, his high will.

    Boyet. Proud of employment, willingly I go.

                                  Exit Boyet.

    Prin. All pride is willing pride, and yours is so.   36
Who are the votaries, my loving lords,
That are vow-fellows with this virtuous duke?

    [A] Lord. Longaville is one.

    Prin.   Know you the man?

    1. Lad. [*Maria*]. I know him, madam: at a marriage
        feast,   40
Between Lord Perigort and the beauteous heir
Of Jacques Falconbridge solemnized,
In Normandy saw I this Longaville.
A man of sovereign parts he is esteem'd;   44
Well fitted in the arts, glorious in arms:
Nothing becomes him ill that he would well.
The only soil of his fair virtue's gloss,—
If virtue's gloss will stain with any soil,—   48
Is a sharp wit match'd with too blunt a will;

25 to's: *to us*
29 best-moving fair: *persuasive and just*
38 duke: *i.e. king* (*cf. I. i.* 180, *I. ii.* 134)
46 would: *i.e. would do*

28 Bold: *confident*
33 attend: *await*
41 Lord Perigort; *cf. n.*
49 blunt: *harsh*

Whose edge hath power to cut, whose will still wills
It should none spare that come within his power.

   Prin. Some merry mocking lord, belike; is 't so?   52

   1. Lad. They say so most that most his humours
     know.

   Prin. Such short-liv'd wits do wither as they grow.
Who are the rest?

   2. Lad. [*Kath.*] The young Dumaine, a well-accom-
     plish'd youth,   56

Of all that virtue love for virtue lov'd:
Most power to do most harm, least knowing ill,
For he hath wit to make an ill shape good,
And shape to win grace though he had no wit.   60
I saw him at the Duke Alençon's once;
And much too little of that good I saw
Is my report to his great worthiness.

   3. Lad. [*Ros.*] Another of these students at that
     time   64

Was there with him, if I have heard a truth.
Berowne they call him; but a merrier man,
Within the limit of becoming mirth,
I never spent an hour's talk withal.   68
His eye begets occasion for his wit;
For every object that the one doth catch
The other turns to a mirth-moving jest,
Which his fair tongue, conceit's expositor,   72
Delivers in such apt and gracious words,
That aged ears play truant at his tales,
And younger hearings are quite ravished;
So sweet and voluble is his discourse.   76

   Prin. God bless my ladies! are they all in love,

50 still: *ever*   57 Of: *by*   59 shape: *form, or figure*
63 report: *testimony; cf. n.*   68 withal: *with*
72 conceit's expositor: *expounder of fancy*   74 *Cf. n.*

That every one her own hath garnished
With such bedecking ornaments of praise?

    [*A*] *Lord.* Here comes Boyet.

Enter Boyet.

    Prin.   Now, what admittance, lord? 80
    Boyet. Navarre had notice of your fair approach;
And he and his competitors in oath
Were all address'd to meet you, gentle lady,
Before I came. Marry, thus much I have learnt;   84
He rather means to lodge you in the field,
Like one that comes here to besiege his court,
Than seek a dispensation for his oath,
To let you enter his unpeopled house.   88

Enter Navarre, Longaville, Dumaine, and Berowne.

Here comes Navarre.

    King. Fair princess, welcome to the court of
      Navarre.

    Prin. 'Fair' I give you back again; and
'welcome' I have not yet: the roof of this court 92
is too high to be yours, and welcome to the wide
fields too base to be mine.

    King. You shall be welcome, madam, to my court.

    Prin. I will be welcome, then: conduct me thither. 96

    King. Hear me, dear lady; I have sworn an oath.

    Prin. Our Lady help my lord! he'll be forsworn.

    King. Not for the world, fair madam, by my will.

    Prin. Why, will shall break it; will, and nothing
      else.   100

    King. Your ladyship is ignorant what it is.

    Prin. Were my lord so, his ignorance were wise,
Where now his knowledge must prove ignorance.

82 competitors: *associates*   83 address'd: *ready*
92 roof of this court: *i.e. the heaven*   103 Where: *whereas*

I hear your grace hath sworn out house-keeping: 104
'Tis deadly sin to keep that oath, my lord,
And sin to break it.
But pardon me, I am too sudden-bold:
To teach a teacher ill beseemeth me.   108
Vouchsafe to read the purpose of my coming,
And suddenly resolve me in my suit. [*Gives a paper.*]

   King. Madam, I will, if suddenly I may.

   Prin. You will the sooner that I were away,   112
For you'll prove perjur'd if you make me stay.

   Ber. Did not I dance with you in Brabant once?

   Ros. Did not I dance with you in Brabant once?

   Ber. I know you did.

   Ros.   How needless was it then 116
To ask the question!

   Ber.   You must not be so quick.

   Ros. 'Tis 'long of you that spur me with such questions.

   Ber. Your wit's too hot, it speeds too fast, 'twill tire.

   Ros. Not till it leave the rider in the mire.   120

   Ber. What time o' day?

   Ros. The hour that fools should ask.

   Ber. Now fair befall your mask!

   Ros. Fair fall the face it covers!   124

   Ber. And send you many lovers!

   Ros. Amen, so you be none.

   Ber. Nay, then will I be gone.

   King. Madam, your father here doth intimate   128
The payment of a hundred thousand crowns;
Being but the one half of an entire sum
Disbursed by my father in his wars.
But say that he, or we,—as neither have,—   132

---

104 sworn out house-keeping: *forsworn hospitality*
110 suddenly: *quickly*   118 'long: *along, because*
123 fair befall: *mercy on*
                                       130 *Cf. n.*

Receiv'd that sum, yet there remains unpaid
A hundred thousand more; in surety of the which,
One part of Aquitaine is bound to us,
Although not valu'd to the money's worth.　　　136
If then the king your father will restore
But that one half which is unsatisfied,
We will give up our right in Aquitaine,
And hold fair friendship with his majesty.　　　140
But that, it seems, he little purposeth,
For here he doth demand to have repaid
A hundred thousand crowns; and not demands,
On payment of a hundred thousand crowns,　　　144
To have his title live in Aquitaine;
Which we much rather had depart withal,
And have the money by our father lent,
Than Aquitaine, so gelded as it is.　　　148
Dear princess, were not his requests so far
From reason's yielding, your fair self should make
A yielding 'gainst some reason in my breast,
And go well satisfied to France again.　　　152

Prin. You do the king my father too much wrong,
And wrong the reputation of your name,
In so unseeming to confess receipt
Of that which hath so faithfully been paid.　　　156

　King. I do protest I never heard of it;
And if you prove it, I'll repay it back
Or yield up Aquitaine.

　　Prin.　　　　　　　We arrest your word.
Boyet, you can produce acquittances　　　160
For such a sum from special officers
Of Charles his father.

　　King.　　　　　　Satisfy me so.

---

146 depart withal: *part with*　　　　　148 gelded: *maimed*
151 A . . . reason: *a rather unreasonable yielding*
155 unseeming: *seeming not*　　　　　159 arrest: *take up, challenge*

　Boyet. So please your Grace, the packet is not come
Where that and other specialties are bound:　164
To-morrow you shall have a sight of them.
　King. It shall suffice me: at which interview
All liberal reason I will yield unto.
Meantime, receive such welcome at my hand　168
As honour, without breach of honour, may
Make tender of to thy true worthiness.
You may not come, fair princess, in my gates;
But here without you shall be so receiv'd,　172
As you shall deem yourself lodg'd in my heart,
Though so denied fair harbour in my house.
Your own good thoughts excuse me, and farewell:
To-morrow shall we visit you again.　176
　Prin. Sweet health and fair desires consort your
　　Grace!
　King. Thy own wish wish I thee in every place!
　　　　　　　　　　　　　　　　Exit [King].
　Ber. Lady, I will commend you to mine own heart.
　Ros. Pray you, do my commendations; I would be
　　glad to see it.　180
　Ber. I would you heard it groan.
　Ros. Is the fool sick?
　Ber. Sick at the heart.
　Ros. Alack! let it blood.　184
　Ber. Would that do it good?
　Ros. My physic says, 'ay.'
　Ber. Will you prick't with your eye?
　Ros. No point, with my knife.　188
　Ber. Now, God save thy life!
　Ros. And yours from long living!

164 specialties: *corroborative documents*
173 As: *that*
184 let it blood; *cf. n.*

177 consort: *accompany*
188 No point; *cf. n.*

Ber. I cannot stay thanksgiving.

                                   Exit [i.e. Retires].

Dum. [*Advancing.*] Sir, I pray you a word: what
    lady is that same?   192

Boyet. The heir of Alençon, Katharine her name.

Dum. A gallant lady. Monsieur, fare you well.

                                         Exit.

Long. I beseech you a word: what is she in the
    white?

Boyet. A woman sometimes, an you saw her in the
    light.   196

Long. Perchance light in the light. I desire her
    name.

Boyet. She hath but one for herself; to desire that
    were a shame.

Long. Pray you, sir, whose daughter?

Boyet. Her mother's, I have heard.   200

Long. God's blessing on your beard!

Boyet. Good sir, be not offended.

She is an heir of Falconbridge.

Long. Nay, my choler is ended.   204

She is a most sweet lady.

Boyet. Not unlike, sir; that may be.

                                 Exit Longaville.

      Enter Berowne [i.e. he advances].

Ber. What's her name, in the cap?

Boyet. Rosaline, by good hap.   208

Ber. Is she wedded or no?

Boyet. To her will, sir, or so.

Ber. You are welcome, sir. Adieu.

---

193 Katharine; *cf. n.*   196 an: *if*
197 light in the light: *of light conduct if known*
201 *Cf. n.*   206 unlike: *unlikely*

Boyet. Farewell to me, sir, and welcome to you.   212
                                    Exit Berowne.

Mar. That last is Berowne, the merry madcap lord:
Not a word with him but a jest.

Boyet.   And every jest but a word.

Prin. It was well done of you to take him at his
   word.

Boyet. I was as willing to grapple, as he was to
   board.   216

Kath. Two hot sheeps, marry!

Boyet.   And wherefore not ships?
No sheep, sweet lamb, unless we feed on your lips.

Kath. You sheep, and I pasture: shall that finish
   the jest?

Boyet. So you grant pasture for me.

                        [*Offering to kiss her.*]

Kath.   Not so, gentle beast. 220
My lips are no common, though several they be.

Boyet. Belonging to whom?

Kath.   To my fortunes and me.

Prin. Good wits will be jangling; but, gentles,
   agree.

This civil war of wits were much better us'd   224
On Navarre and his book-men, for here 'tis abus'd.

Boyet. If my observation,—which very seldom lies,
By the heart's still rhetoric disclosed with eyes,—
Deceive me not now, Navarre is infected.   228

Prin. With what?

Boyet. With that which we lovers entitle affected.

Prin. Your reason.

Boyet. Why, all his behaviours did make their re-
   tire   232

212 *Cf. n.*   217 Kath.; *cf. n.*
221 common, though several; *cf. n.*   225 abus'd: *misused*
227 rhetoric: *language*   230 affected: *loving, sentimental*

To the court of his eye, peeping thorough desire.
His heart, like an agate, with your print impress'd,
Proud with his form, in his eye pride express'd.
His tongue, all impatient to speak and not see,   236
Did stumble with haste in his eyesight to be;
All senses to that sense did make their repair,
To feel only looking on fairest of fair:
Methought all his senses were lock'd in his eye,   240
As jewels in crystal for some prince to buy;
Who, tend'ring their own worth from where they were
          glass'd,
Did point you to buy them, along as you pass'd.
His face's own margent did quote such amazes,   244
That all eyes saw his eyes enchanted with gazes.
I'll give you Aquitaine, and all that is his,
An you give him for my sake but one loving kiss.
    Prin. Come to our pavilion: Boyet is dispos'd.   248
    Boyet. But to speak that in words which his eye
      hath disclos'd.
I only have made a mouth of his eye,
By adding a tongue which I know will not lie.
    Ros. Thou art an old love-monger, and speak'st
      skilfully.   252
    Mar. He is Cupid's grandfather, and learns news of
      him.
    Kath. Then was Venus like her mother, for her
      father is but grim.
    Boyet. Do you hear, my mad wenches?
    Ros.   No.
    Boyet.   What, then, do you see?

233 court: *governing center*   235 with his: *with its*
236 to speak and not see: *not to be able to see rather than to speak*
239 To feel only looking: *that they might feel only in looking*
243 point: *invite*   244 margent: *margin; cf. n.*   quote: *note*
248 dispos'd: *inclined to be merry*   249 But: *i.e. disposed only*

Ros. Ay, our way to be gone.
Boyet.   You are too hard for me. 256
                                        Exeunt Omnes.

ACT THIRD

Scene One

[The King of Navarre's Park]

Enter Braggart [Armado] and his Boy [Moth].

Arm. Warble, child; make passionate my sense of hearing.

Moth. [*Singing.*] Concolinel,—

Arm. Sweet air! Go, tenderness of years; 4 take this key, give enlargement to the swain, bring him festinately hither; I must employ him in a letter to my love.

Moth. Master, will you win your love with a 8 French brawl?

Arm. How meanest thou? brawling in French?

Moth. No, my complete master; but to jig off 12 a tune at the tongue's end, canary to it with your feet, humour it with turning up your eyelids, sigh a note and sing a note, sometime through the throat, [as] if you swallowed love by singing 16 love, sometime through [the] nose, as if you snuffed up love by smelling love; with your hat penthouse-like o'er the shop of your eyes; with your arms crossed on your thin belly-doublet like a 20

3 Concolinel; *cf. n.*
9 brawl: *dance; cf. n.*
18 penthouse-like: *porch-like*

6 festinately: *quickly*
13 canary: *dance; cf. n.*

rabbit on a spit; or your hands in your pocket like a man after the old painting; and keep not too long in one tune, but a snip and away. These are complements, these are humours, these be- 24 tray nice wenches, that would be betrayed without these; and make them men of note,—do you note? men,—that most are affected to these.

Arm. How hast thou purchased this ex- 28 perience?

Moth. By my penny of observation.

Arm. But O—but O,—

Moth. 'The hobby-horse is forgot.' 32

Arm. Callest thou my love 'hobby-horse'?

Moth. No, master; the hobby-horse is but a colt, and your love perhaps a hackney. But have you forgot your love? 36

Arm. Almost I had.

Moth. Negligent student! learn her by heart.

Arm. By heart, and in heart, boy.

Moth. And out of heart, master: all those 40 three I will prove.

Arm. What wilt thou prove?

Moth. A man, if I live; and this, by, in, and without, upon the instant: by heart you love 44 her, because your heart cannot come by her; in heart you love her, because your heart is in love with her; and out of heart you love her, being out of heart that you cannot enjoy her. 48

Arm. I am all these three.

Moth. And three times as much more, and yet nothing at all.

24 complements: *accomplishments*   25 nice: *coy*
30 penny: *i.e. purchasing medium*   32 *Cf. n.*
35 hackney: *i.e. loose woman*

Arm. Fetch hither the swain: he must carry 52
me a letter.

Moth. A message well sympathized: a horse
to be ambassador for an ass.

Arm. Ha, ha! what sayest thou?   56

Moth. Marry, sir, you must send the ass upon
the horse, for he is very slow-gaited. But I go.

Arm. The way is but short: away!

Moth. As swift as lead, sir.   60

Arm. The meaning, pretty ingenious?
Is not lead a metal heavy, dull, and slow?

Moth. Minime, honest master; or rather, master, no.

Arm. I say, lead is slow.

Moth.   You are too swift, sir, to say so. 64
Is that lead slow which is fir'd from a gun?

Arm. Sweet smoke of rhetoric!
He reputes me a cannon; and the bullet, that's he:
I shoot thee at the swain.

Moth.   Thump, then, and I flee. 68
          [*Exit.*]

Arm. A most acute juvenal; volable and free of
          grace!
By thy favour, sweet welkin, I must sigh in thy face:
Most rude melancholy, valour gives thee place.
My herald is return'd.   72

     Enter Page [*Moth*] *and Clown* [*Costard*].

Moth. A wonder, master! here's a costard broken
in a shin.

Arm. Some enigma, some riddle: come, thy *l'envoy;*
begin.

Cost. No egma, no riddle, no *l'envoy;* no salve

54 well sympathized: *i.e. the message is well suited to the bearer*
63 Minime: *by no means*   68 Thump: *bang!*
69 volable: *quick of wit*   70 welkin: *sky*   73 costard: *head*

in the mail, sir.   O! sir, plantain, a plain plan- 76
tain: no *l'envoy*, no *l'envoy*: no salve, sir, but a
plantain.

  Arm. By virtue, thou enforcest laughter; thy
silly thought, my spleen; the heaving of my 80
lungs provokes me to ridiculous smiling: O!
pardon me, my stars.   Doth the inconsiderate
take salve for *l'envoy*, and the word *l'envoy* for
a salve?   84

  Moth. Do the wise think them other? is not
l'envoy a salve?

  Arm. No, page: it is an epilogue or discourse, to
  make plain
Some obscure precedence that hath tofore been sain. 88
I will example it:

        The fox, the ape, and the humble-bee
        Were still at odds, being but three.
There's the moral. Now the *l'envoy*.   92

  Moth. I will add the l'envoy. Say the moral
again.

  Arm. The fox, the ape, and the humble-bee
        Were still at odds, being but three.   96

Moth. Until the goose came out of door,
        And stay'd the odds by adding four.
Now will I begin your moral, and do you follow
with my *l'envoy*.   100

        The fox, the ape, and the humble-bee
        Were still at odds, being but three.

'*Arm.* Until the goose came out of door,
        Staying the odds by adding four.   104

  Moth. A good *l'envoy*, ending in the goose.
Would you desire more?

76 mail: *bag; cf. n.*   80 spleen: *mirth*
86 l'envoy a salve; *cf. n.*   88 sain: *said*
98 adding: *i.e. making*

Cost. The boy hath sold him a bargain, a goose, that's flat.
Sir, your pennyworth is good, an your goose be fat. 108
To sell a bargain well is as cunning as fast and loose.
Let me see: a fat *l'envoy;* ay, that's a fat goose.

Arm. Come hither, come hither. How did this argument begin?

Moth. By saying that a costard was broken in a shin.   112
Then call'd you for the *l'envoy.*

Cost. True, and I for a plantain: thus came your argument in;
Then the boy's fat *l'envoy,* the goose that you bought;
And he ended the market.   116

Arm. But tell me: how was there a costard broken in a shin?

Moth. I will tell you sensibly.

Cost. Thou hast no feeling of it, Moth: I will 120 speak that *l'envoy:*
I, Costard, running out, that was safely within,
Fell over the threshold and broke my shin.

Arm. We will talk no more of this matter.   124

Cost. Till there be more matter in the shin.

Arm. Sirrah Costard, I will enfranchise thee.

Cost. O! marry me to one Frances: I smell some *l'envoy,* some goose, in this.   128

Arm. By my sweet soul, I mean setting thee at liberty, enfreedoming thy person: thou wert immured, restrained, captivated, bound.

Cost. True, true, and now you will be my pur- 132 gation and let me loose.

Arm. I give thee thy liberty, set thee from

107 hath . . . bargain; *cf. n.*   116 market; *cf. n.*
119 sensibly: *feelingly*

durance; and in lieu thereof, impose on thee
nothing but this:—[*Giving a letter.*] Bear this 136
significant to the country maid Jaquenetta.
[*Giving money.*] There is remuneration; for
the best ward of mine honour is rewarding my
dependents.　Moth, follow.　　　　　[*Exit.*]

Moth. Like the sequel, I.　Signior Costard, adieu.

　　　　　　　　　　　　　　　　　　　Exit.

Cost. My sweet ounce of man's flesh! my incony
　　Jew!—

Now will I look to his remuneration.　Remuneration! O that's the Latin word for three far- 144
things: three farthings, remuneration.　'What's
the price of this inkle?' 'One penny.' 'No, I'll
give you a remuneration': why, it carries it.
Remuneration! why, it is a fairer name than 148
French crown.　I will never buy and sell out of
this word.

　　　　　　　Enter Berowne.

　Ber. O my good knave Costard, exceedingly
well met!　　　　　　　　　　　　　　　152

　Cost. Pray you, sir, how much carnation
ribbon may a man buy for a remuneration?

　Ber. What is a remuneration?

　Cost. Marry, sir, halfpenny farthing.　　156

　Ber. Oh! Why then, three-farthing-worth of silk.

　Cost. I thank your worship.　God be wi'
you!

Ber. O stay, slave; I must employ thee.　　160
As thou wilt win my favour, good my knave,
Do one thing for me that I shall entreat.

---

137 significant: *token, i.e. letter*　　139 ward: *guard*
142 incony: *fine*　　　　　　　　　146 inkle: *tape*
147 it carries it: *it carries off the palm*　148 name: *word*
158 wi': *with*

Cost. When would you have it done, sir?

Ber. O, this afternoon.   164

Cost. Well, I will do it, sir. Fare you well.

Ber. O, thou knowest not what it is.

Cost. I shall know, sir, when I have done it.

Ber. Why, villain, thou must know first.   168

Cost. I will come to your worship to-morrow
morning.

Ber. It must be done this afternoon.   Hark,
slave, it is but this: 172

The princess comes to hunt here in the park,

And in her train there is a gentle lady:

When tongues speak sweetly, then they name her
name,

And Rosaline they call her: ask for her   176

And to her white hand see thou do commend

This seal'd-up counsel. [*Gives him a shilling.*] There's
thy guerdon: go.

Cost. Gardon, O sweet gardon! better than
remuneration; a 'leven-pence farthing better. 180

Most sweet gardon! I will do it, sir, in print.

Gardon! remuneration!   *Exit.*

Ber. O! And I,—

Forsooth, in love! I, that have been love's whip;   184

A very beadle to a humorous sigh;

A critic, nay, a night-watch constable,

A domineering pedant o'er the boy,

Than whom no mortal so magnificent!   188

This wimpled, whining, purblind, wayward boy,

This senior-junior, giant-dwarf, Dan Cupid;

Regent of love-rimes, lord of folded arms,

---

178 counsel: *private communication*   guerdon: *reward*
181 in print: *precisely*   185 beadle . . . sigh; *cf. n.*
188 magnificent: *pompous, overbearing*
189 wimpled: *veiled*   purblind: *totally blind*   190 *Cf. n.*

The anointed sovereign of sighs and groans,   192
Liege of all loiterers and malcontents,
Dread prince of plackets, king of codpieces,
Sole imperator and great general
Of trotting 'paritors: O my little heart!   196
And I to be a corporal of his field,
And wear his colours like a tumbler's hoop!
What! I love! I sue! I seek a wife!
A woman that is like a German clock,   200
Still a-repairing, ever out of frame,
And never going aright, being a watch,
But being watch'd that it may still go right!
Nay, to be perjur'd, which is worst of all;   204
And, among three, to love the worst of all;
A whitely wanton with a velvet brow,
With two pitch balls stuck in her face for eyes.
Ay, and, by heaven, one that will do the deed,   208
Though Argus were her eunuch and her guard.
And I to sigh for her! to watch for her!
To pray for her! Go to: it is a plague
That Cupid will impose for my neglect   212
Of his almighty dreadful little might.
Well, I will love, write, sigh, pray, sue, groan:
Some men must love my lady, and some Joan.

                                                [Exit.]

194 plackets: *petticoats, or slits in petticoats or skirts*   codpieces: *baggy appendages to the front of breeches*
196 'paritors: *apparitors, officials of the ecclesiastical court*
198 like . . . hoop: *like the flaunting ribbons attached to a tumbler's
hoop*   201 frame: *order*
206 whitely: *pale-skinned*
209 Argus: *a monster having a hundred eyes*
215 Joan: *stock name for a peasant wench; cf. IV. iii. 182 and
V. ii. 928*

ACT FOURTH

Scene One

[The King of Navarre's Park]

Enter the Princess, a Forester, her Ladies, and her Lords.

Prin. Was that the king, that spurr'd his horse so
  hard
Against the steep uprising of the hill?
  Boyet. I know not; but I think it was not he.
  Prin. Whoe'er a' was, a' show'd a mounting mind. 4
Well, lords, to-day we shall have our dispatch;
On Saturday we will return to France.
Then, forester, my friend, where is the bush
That we must stand and play the murtherer in?   8
  For. Hereby, upon the edge of yonder coppice;
A stand where you may make the fairest shoot.
  Prin. I thank my beauty, I am fair that shoot,
And thereupon thou speak'st the fairest shoot.   12
  For. Pardon me, madam, for I meant not so.
  Prin. What, what? first praise me, and again say no?
O short-liv'd pride! Not fair? alack for woe!
  For. Yes, madam, fair.
  Prin.   Nay, never paint me now: 16
Where fair is not, praise cannot mend the brow.
Here, good my glass.—[*Gives money.*] Take this for
  telling true:
Fair payment for foul words is more than due.
  For. Nothing but fair is that which you inherit. 20
  Prin. See, see! my beauty will be sav'd by merit.

9 coppice: *thicket*   10 stand: *hunter's station*
17 fair: *beauty*   18 my glass: *mirror, i.e. the Forester*
20 inherit: *possess*   21 merit: *good deeds*

O heresy in fair, fit for these days!
A giving hand, though foul, shall have fair praise.
But come, the bow: now mercy goes to kill,   24
And shooting well is then accounted ill.
Thus will I save my credit in the shoot:
Not wounding, pity would not let me do 't;
If wounding, then it was to show my skill,   28
That more for praise than purpose meant to kill.
And out of question so it is sometimes,
Glory grows guilty of detested crimes,
When, for fame's sake, for praise, an outward part, 32
We bend to that the working of the heart;
As I for praise alone now seek to spill
The poor deer's blood, that my heart means no ill.

   Boyet. Do not curst wives hold that self-sover-
     eignty   36
Only for praise' sake, when they strive to be
Lords o'er their lords?

   Prin. Only for praise; and praise we may afford
To any lady that subdues a lord.   40

Enter Clown [Costard].

   Boyet. Here comes a member of the commonwealth.

   Cost. God dig-you-den all! Pray you, which
is the head lady?

   Prin. Thou shalt know her, fellow, by the 44
rest that have no heads.

   Cost. Which is the greatest lady, the highest?

   Prin. The thickest, and the tallest.

   Cost. The thickest, and the tallest: it is so; truth
is truth.   48

22 heresy; *cf. n.*   23 giving: *generous*
30 out of question: *undoubtedly*
32 outward part: *extraneous quality*   36 curst: *shrewish*
41 commonwealth: *i.e. common people*
42 dig-you-den: *give you good evening*   48 The thickest, etc.: *cf. n*

An your waist, mistress, were as slender as my wit,
One o' these maids' girdles for your waist should be
    fit.
Are not you the chief woman? you are the thickest
    here.
    Prin. What's your will, sir? what's your will?   52
    Cost. I have a letter from Monsieur Berowne to one
        Lady Rosaline.
    Prin. O thy letter, thy letter! He's a good friend
        of mine.
Stand aside, good bearer. Boyet, you can carve;
Break up this capon.
    Boyet.   I am bound to serve.—   56
This letter is mistook; it importeth none here:
It is writ to Jaquenetta.
    Prin.   We will read it, I swear.
Break the neck of the wax, and every one give ear.
    Boyet. [*Reads.*] 'By heaven, that thou art fair, 60
is most infallible; true, that thou art beauteous;
truth itself, that thou art lovely. More fairer than
fair, beautiful than beauteous, truer than truth
itself, have commiseration on thy heroical vas- 64
sal. The magnanimous and most illustrate
king Cophetua set eye upon the pernicious and
indubitate beggar Zenelophon, and he it was
that might rightly say *veni, vidi, vici;* which to 68
anatomize in the vulgar—O base and obscure
vulgar!—*videlicet,* he came, saw, and overcame:
he came, one; saw, two; overcame, three. Who
came? the king: Why did he come? to see: Why 72
did he see? to overcome: To whom came he? to

56 capon: *love-letter; cf. n.*   57 importeth: *concerns*
65 illustrate: *illustrious*
67 indubitate: *indubitable*   Zenelophon: *Penelophon (in the old*
    ballad)   69 anatomize: *analyze, explain*

the beggar: What saw he? the beggar.   Who
overcame he? the beggar.   The conclusion is
victory: on whose side? the king's; the captive 76
is enriched: on whose side? the beggar's.   The
catastrophe is a nuptial: on whose side? the
king's, no, on both in one, or one in both.   I am
the king, for so stands the comparison; thou 80
the beggar, for so witnesseth thy lowliness.   Shall
I command thy love? I may: Shall I enforce
thy love? I could: Shall I entreat thy love? I
will.   What shalt thou exchange for rags? robes; 84
for tittles? titles; for thyself? me.   Thus, expecting thy reply, I profane my lips on thy foot,
my eyes on thy picture, and my heart on thy
every part.   88

    Thine, in the dearest design of Industry,
                    Don Adriano de Armado.

Thus dost thou hear the Nemean lion roar
'Gainst thee, thou lamb, that standest as his prey: 92
Submissive fall his princely feet before,
    And he from forage will incline to play.
But if thou strive, poor soul, what art thou then?
Food for his rage, repasture for his den.'   96

    Prin. What plume of feathers is he that indited this
        letter?
What vane? what weathercock? did you ever hear
        better?
    Boyet. I am much deceiv'd but I remember the style.
    Prin. Else your memory is bad, going o'er it ere-
        while.   100

85 expecting: *awaiting*   89 Industry: *gallantry*
91 Nemean lion; *cf. n.*   94 from forage: *abandoning rapacity*
96 repasture: *repast*   97 plume of feathers: *featherhead*
99 but: *unless*   100 erewhile: *just now*

Boyet. This Armado is a Spaniard, that keeps here
   in court;
A phantasime, a Monarcho, and one that makes sport
To the prince and his book-mates.
   Prin.   Thou fellow, a word.
Who gave thee this letter?
   Cost.   I told you; my lord. 104
   Prin. To whom shouldst thou give it?
   Cost.   From my lord to my lady.
   Prin. From which lord, to which lady?
   Cost. From my lord Berowne, a good master of
   mine,
To a lady of France, that he call'd Rosaline.   108
   Prin. Thou hast mistaken his letter. Come, lords,
   away.
Here, sweet, put up this: 'twill be thine another day.
                    Exeunt [Princess and Train].
   Boyet. Who is the suitor? who is the suitor?
   Ros.   Shall I teach you to know?
   Boyet. Ay, my continent of beauty.
   Ros.   Why, she that bears the bow. 112
Finely put off!
   Boyet. My lady goes to kill horns; but, if thou
   marry,
Hang me by the neck if horns that year miscarry.
Finely put on!   116
   Ros. Well then, I am the shooter.
   Boyet.   And who is your deer?
   Ros. If we choose by the horns, yourself: come not
   near.
Finely put on, indeed!

101 keeps: *lives*
102 phantasime: *fantastic fellow*   Monarcho; *cf. n.*
110 sweet: *i.e. Rosaline*   be thine: *be of use to thee*
112 continent: *container, repository*   bears the bow; *cf. n.*
113 put off: *turned aside*   115 horns; *cf. n.*

Mar. You still wrangle with her, Boyet, and she
    strikes at the brow.   120

Boyet. But she herself is hit lower. Have I hit her
    now?

    Ros. Shall I come upon thee with an old say-
ing, that was a man when King Pepin of France
was a little boy, as touching the hit it?   124

    Boyet. So I may answer thee with one as
old, that was a woman when Queen Guinever
of Britain was a little wench, as touching the
hit it.   128

Ros.   'Thou canst not hit it, hit it, hit it,
          Thou canst not hit it, my good man.

Boyet.   'An I cannot, cannot, cannot,
          An I cannot, another can.'   132

                     Exit [*Rosaline*].

Cost. By my troth, most pleasant: how both did
    fit it!

Mar. A mark marvellous well shot, for they both
    did hit it.

Boyet. A mark! O mark but that mark; a mark,
    says my lady!

Let the mark have a prick in 't, to mete at, if it may
    be.   136

Mar. Wide o' the bow hand! i' faith your hand is
    out.

Cost. Indeed a' must shoot nearer, or he'll ne'er hit
    the clout.

Boyet. An if my hand be out, then belike your hand
    is in.

120 still: *ever*   123 King Pepin; *cf. n.*
133 fit it: *make their points*
136 prick: *point in the center of the target*   mete: *measure, aim*
137 Wide . . . hand: *too far to the left*
138 clout: *white mark of cloth in the center of the target*

Cost. Then will she get the upshoot by cleaving the
  pin.   140

Mar. Come, come, you talk greasily; your lips
  grow foul.

Cost. She's too hard for you at pricks, sir: challenge
  her to bowl.

Boyet. I fear too much rubbing. Good night, my
  good owl.   *[Exeunt Boyet and Maria.]*

Cost. By my soul, a swain! a most simple clown! 144
Lord, lord, how the ladies and I have put him down!
O' my troth, most sweet jests! most incony vulgar wit!
When it comes so smoothly off, so obscenely, as it
  were, so fit.
Armado, o' the one side, O! a most dainty man.   148
To see him walk before a lady, and to bear her fan!
To see him kiss his hand! and how most sweetly a'
  will swear!
And his page o' t'other side, that handful of wit!
Ah! heavens, it is a most pathetical nit.   *Shout within.*
Sola, sola!   *[Exit running.]*

Scene Two

[The Same]

Enter Dull, Holofernes the Pedant, and Nathaniel.

Nath. Very reverend sport, truly: and done
in the testimony of a good conscience.

Hol. The deer was, as you know, *sanguis,* in
blood; ripe as the pomewater, who now hangeth 4
like a jewel in the ear of *cœlo,* the sky, the welkin,

---

140 upshoot: *upshot, leading shot in a competition*   pin: *wooden
  pin holding up the clout*   141 greasily: *grossly*
142 bowl: *bowling*   152 pathetical nit: *pleasing little fellow*
4 pomewater: *a kind of apple*

the heaven; and anon falleth like a crab on the
face of *terra,* the soil, the land, the earth.

Nath. Truly, Master Holofernes, the epithets 8
are sweetly varied, like a scholar at the least: but,
sir, I assure ye, it was a buck of the first head.

Hol. Sir Nathaniel, *haud credo.*

Dull. 'Twas not a *haud credo;* 'twas a pricket. 12

Hol. Most barbarous intimation! yet a kind
of insinuation, as it were, *in via,* in way, of ex-
plication; *facere,* as it were, replication, or,
rather, *ostentare,* to show, as it were, his inclina- 16
tion,—after his undressed, unpolished, unedu-
cated, unpruned, untrained, or, rather, unlettered, or, ratherest, unconfirmed fashion,—to
insert again my *haud credo* for a deer.   20

Dull. I said the deer was not a *haud credo;*
'twas a pricket.

Hol. Twice sod simplicity, *bis coctus!*

O thou monster Ignorance, how deformed dost thou
    look!   24

Nath. Sir, he hath not fed of the dainties that are
    bred in a book.

He hath not eat paper, as it were; he hath not
drunk ink: his intellect is not replenished; he is
only an animal, only sensible in the duller parts: 28

And such barren plants are set before us, that we
    thankful should be,

Which we [of] taste and feeling are, for those parts
    that do fructify in us more than he;

10 first head: *fifth year*   11 haud credo: *I do not think so*
12 pricket: *buck of the second year*
15 facere . . . replication: *to make reply*
19 unconfirmed: *ignorant*
23 sod: *sodden*   bis coctus: *twice cooked, insipid*
30 Which we: *we who*   than he: *i.e. than in him*

For as it would ill become me to be vain, indiscreet,
or a fool:

So were there a patch set on learning, to see him in a
school: 32

But, *omne bene,* say I; being of an old Father's mind,

Many can brook the weather that love not the wind.

   Dull. You two are book-men: can you tell me by
your wit,

What was a month old at Cain's birth, that's not five
weeks old as yet?   36

   Hol. Dictynna, goodman Dull: Dictynna, goodman
Dull.

   Dull. What is Dictynna?

   Nath. A title to Phœbe, to Luna, to the moon.

   Hol. The moon was a month old when Adam was
no more;   40

And raught not to five weeks when he came to five-
score.

The allusion holds in the exchange.

   Dull. 'Tis true indeed: the collusion holds in the
exchange.

   Hol. God comfort thy capacity! I say, the 44
allusion holds in the exchange.

   Dull. And I say the pollution holds in the
exchange, for the moon is never but a month old;
and I say beside that 'twas a pricket that the 48
princess killed.

   Hol. Sir Nathaniel, will you hear an extemporal epitaph on the death of the deer? and, to
humour the ignorant, [I have] call'd the deer the 52
princess killed, a pricket.

---

32 patch: *clown, fool; cf. n.*   33 omne bene: *all's well*
34 *Cf. n.*   37 Dictynna: *a name given to Diana; cf. n.*
41 raught: *reached*   42 allusion: *jest, riddle; cf. n.*
50 extemporal: *extemporary*

Nath. Perge, good Master Holofernes, *perge;*
so it shall please you to abrogate scurrility.

Hol. I will something affect the letter; for it 56
argues facility.

'The preyful princess pierc'd and prick'd a pretty
   pleasing pricket;

Some say a sore; but not a sore, till now made sore
   with shooting.

The dogs did yell; put L to sore, then sorel jumps
   from thicket;   60

Or pricket, sore, or else sorel; the people fall a
   hooting.

If sore be sore, then L to sore makes fifty sores one
   sorel!

Of one sore I a hundred make, by adding but one
   more L.'

Nath. A rare talent!   64

Dull. [*Aside.*] If a talent be a claw, look how
he claws him with a talent.

Hol. This is a gift that I have, simple, simple;
a foolish extravagant spirit, full of forms, figures, 68
shapes, objects, ideas, apprehensions, motions,
revolutions. These are begot in the ventricle of
memory, nourished in the womb of *pia mater,*
and delivered upon the mellowing of occasion. 72
But the gift is good in those in whom it is acute,
and I am thankful for it.

Nath. Sir, I praise the Lord for you, and so
may my parishioners; for their sons are well 76
tutored by you, and their daughters profit very

54 Perge: *proceed*   56 affect the letter: *make use of alliteration*
59 sore: *a deer of the fourth year*
60 sorel: *a deer of the third year*   65 talent: *talon*
66 claws: *scratches pleasantly, flatters*
70 ventricle: *a division of the brain here called pia mater*

greatly under you: you are a good member of the commonwealth.

Hol. Mehercle! if their sons be ingenuous, they 80 shall want no instruction; if their daughters be capable, I will put it to them. But, *vir sapit qui pauca loquitur.* A soul feminine saluteth us.

Enter Jaquenetta and the Clown [Costard].

Jaq. God give you good morrow, Master parson. 84

Hol. Master parson, *quasi* pers-on? And if one should be pierced, which is the one?

Cost. Marry, Master schoolmaster, he that is likest to a hogshead. 88

Hol. Of piercing a hogshead! a good lustre of conceit in a turf of earth; fire enough for a flint, pearl enough for a swine: 'tis pretty; it is well.

Jaq. Good Master parson [*giving a letter to* 92 *Nathaniel*], be so good as read me this letter: it was given me by Costard, and sent me from Don Armado: I beseech you, read it.

Hol. Fauste, precor gelida quando pecus 96 *omne sub umbra Ruminat,* and so forth. Ah! good old Mantuan. I may speak of thee as the traveller doth of Venice:

    —Venetia, Venetia,   100
     Chi non te vede, non te pretia.

Old Mantuan! old Mantuan! Who understandeth thee not, loves thee not. *Ut, re, sol, la, mi, fa.* Under pardon, sir, what are the con- 104 tents? or, rather, as Horace says in his—What, my soul, verses?

---

80 Mehercle: *a small oath*   82 vir sapit, etc.; *cf. n.*
86 pierced: *pronounced 'persed'*   89 Of: *in reference to*
96-98 Fauste . . . Mantuan; *cf. n.*
100, 101 Venetia . . . pretia; *cf. n.*
103, 104 Ut . . . fa; *cf. n.*
                                                105 Horace; *cf. n.*

Nath. Ay, sir, and very learned.

Hol. Let me hear a staff, a stanze, a verse: 108
lege, domine.

Nath. 'If love make me forsworn, how shall I swear
to love?

Ah! never faith could hold, if not to beauty vow'd;

Though to myself forsworn, to thee I'll faithful
prove;   112

Those thoughts to me were oaks, to thee like osiers
bow'd.

Study his bias leaves and makes his book thine eyes,

Where all those pleasures live that art would com-
prehend:

If knowledge be the mark, to know thee shall
suffice.   116

Well learned is that tongue that well can thee commend;

All ignorant that soul that sees thee without wonder;

Which is to me some praise, that I thy parts admire.

Thy eye Jove's lightning bears, thy voice his dreadful
thunder,   120

Which, not to anger bent, is music and sweet fire.

Celestial as thou art, O pardon love this wrong,

That sings heaven's praise with such an earthly
tongue!'

Hol. You find not the apostrophas, and so 124
miss the accent: let me supervise the canzonet.
Here are only numbers ratified; but, for the
elegancy, facility, and golden cadence of poesy,
caret. Ovidius Naso was the man: and why, 128
indeed, Naso, but for smelling out the odori-

109 lege, domine: *read, master*
114 his bias: *i.e. its natural tendency*
124 apostrophas: *apostrophes; cf. n.*   126 numbers ratified; *cf. n.*
128 caret: *it is wanting*   129 Naso: *from 'nasus,' nose*

ferous flowers of fancy, the jerks of invention?
Imitari is nothing; so doth the hound his
master, the ape his keeper, the tired horse his 132
rider. But, damosella virgin, was this directed
to you?

Jaq. Ay, sir; from one Monsieur Berowne,
one of the strange queen's lords.   136

Hol. I will overglance the superscript. *'To
the snow-white hand of the most beauteous
Lady Rosaline.'* I will look again on the intellect of the letter, for the nomination of the party 140
writing to the person written unto: *'Your ladyship's, in all desired employment, Berowne.'*—
Sir Nathaniel, this Berowne is one of the votaries
with the king; and here he hath framed a letter 144
to a sequent of the stranger queen's, which, accidentally, or by the way of progression, hath mis-
carried. Trip and go, my sweet; deliver this
paper into the royal hand of the king; it may 148
concern much. Stay not thy compliment; I
forgive thy duty: adieu.

Jaq. Good Costard, go with me. Sir, God
save your life!   152

Cost. Have with thee, my girl.

                 Exit [with Jaquenetta].

Nath. Sir, you have done this in the fear of
God, very religiously; and, as a certain Father
saith—   156

Hol. Sir, tell not me of the Father; I do fear
colourable colours. But to return to the verses:
did they please you, Sir Nathaniel?

131 Imitari: *to imitate*   136 queen's lords; *cf. n.*
137 superscript: *superscription, address*   139 intellect: *i.e. signature*
145 sequent: *follower*   147 Trip and go; *cf. n.*
149 Stay . . . compliment: *do not pause for ceremony*
158 colourable colours: *false pretexts*

Nath. Marvellous well for the pen.   160

Hol. I do dine to-day at the father's of a
certain pupil of mine; where, if before repast it
shall please you to gratify the table with a grace,
I will, on my privilege I have with the parents 164
of the foresaid child or pupil, undertake your
ben venuto; where I will prove those verses to
be very unlearned, neither savouring of poetry,
wit, nor invention.   I beseech your society.   168

Nath. And thank you too; for society—saith
the text—is the happiness of life.

Hol. And, certes, the text most infallibly concludes it.—[*To Dull.*] Sir, I do invite you too: 172
you shall not say me nay: *pauca verba*.   Away!
the gentles are at their game, and we will to our
recreation.   *Exeunt.*

Scene Three

[*The Same*]

Enter Berowne, with a paper in his hand, alone.

Ber. The king he is hunting the deer; I am
coursing myself: they have pitched a toil; I am
toiling in a pitch,—pitch that defiles: defile! a
foul word!   Well, sit thee down, sorrow! for so 4
they say the fool said, and so say I, and I the
fool: well proved, wit!   By the Lord, this love is
as mad as Ajax: it kills sheep: it kills me, I a
sheep: well proved again o' my side!   I will not 8
love; if I do, hang me; i' faith, I will not.   O

---

160 pen: *technical skill*   166 ben venuto: *welcome*
170 the text; *cf. n.*   173 pauca verba: *few words*
2 pitched a toil: *set a net*   3 pitch: *i.e. Rosaline's black eyes*
7 Ajax; *cf. n.*

but her eye!—by this light, but for her eye, I
would not love her; yes, for her two eyes. Well,
I do nothing in the world but lie, and lie in my 12
throat. By heaven, I do love, and it hath
taught me to rime, and to be melancholy; and
here is part of my rime, and here my melancholy. Well, she hath one o' my sonnets al- 16
ready: the clown bore it, the fool sent it, and
the lady hath it: sweet clown, sweeter fool,
sweetest lady! By the world, I would not care a
pin if the other three were in. Here comes one 20
with a paper: God give him grace to groan!

He stands aside [or climbs into a tree].

The King entreth.

King. Ay me!
Ber. [*Aside.*] Shot, by heaven! Proceed,
sweet Cupid: thou hast thumped him with 24
thy bird-bolt under the left pap. In faith,
secrets!
King. 'So sweet a kiss the golden sun gives not
To those fresh morning drops upon the rose,   28
As thy eye-beams, when their fresh rays have smote
The night of dew that on my cheeks down flows.
Nor shines the silver moon one half so bright
Through the transparent bosom of the deep,   32
As doth thy face through tears of mine give light:
Thou shin'st in every tear that I do weep;
No drop but as a coach doth carry thee:
So ridest thou triumphing in my woe.   36
Do but behold the tears that swell in me,
And they thy glory through my grief will show:
But do not love thyself; then thou wilt keep

20 in: *i.e. in love*   25 bird-bolt: *blunt arrow for killing birds*

My tears for glasses, and still make me weep.   40
O queen of queens! how far dost thou excel,
No thought can think, nor tongue of mortal tell.'
How shall she know my griefs? I'll drop the paper.—
Sweet leaves, shade folly! Who is he comes here? 44

    Enter Longaville. The King steps aside.

What, Longaville! and reading! listen, ear.
   Ber. Now, in thy likeness, one more fool appear!
   Long. Ay me! I am forsworn.
   Ber. Why, he comes in like a perjure, wearing
      papers.   48
   King. In love, I hope: sweet fellowship in shame!
   Ber. One drunkard loves another of the name.
   Long. Am I the first that have been perjur'd so?
   Ber. I could put thee in comfort: not by two that I
      know: 52
Thou mak'st the triumviry, the corner-cap of society,
The shape of love's Tyburn, that hangs up simplicity.
   Long. I fear these stubborn lines lack power to
      move.
O sweet Maria, empress of my love!   56
These numbers will I tear, and write in prose.
   Ber. O! rimes are guards on wanton Cupid's hose:
Disfigure not his slop.
   Long.   This same shall go.
                          He reads the Sonnet.
'Did not the heavenly rhetoric of thine eye,   60
   'Gainst whom the world cannot hold argument,
Persuade my heart to this false perjury?

48 perjure: *perjurer*   papers: *papers on the breast describing a
    perjurer's offenses*
53 triumviry: *triumvirate*   corner-cap: *biretta, three-cornered cap,
    of a Catholic priest*
54 Tyburn: *triangular gallows at Tyburn, London*
58 guards: *trimmings*   59 slop: *loose trousers*

Vows for thee broke deserve not punishment.
A woman I forswore; but I will prove,   64
   Thou being a goddess, I forswore not thee:
My vow was earthly, thou a heavenly love;
   Thy grace, being gain'd, cures all disgrace in me.
Vows are but breath, and breath a vapour is: 68
   Then thou, fair sun, which on my earth dost shine,
Exhal'st this vapour-vow; in thee it is:
   If broken, then, it is no fault of mine:
If by me broke, what fool is not so wise   72
To lose an oath to win a paradise!'

   Ber. This is the liver-vein, which makes flesh a
     dcity,
A green goose a goddess; pure, pure idolatry.
God amend us, God amend! we are much out o' the
   way.   76

   Long. By whom shall I send this?—Company! stay.
                           [Steps aside.]

              Enter Dumaine.

   Ber. All hid, all hid; an old infant play.
Like a demi-god here sit I in the sky,
And wretched fools' secrets heedfully o'er-eye.   80
More sacks to the mill! O heavens! I have my wish.
Dumaine transform'd: four woodcocks in a dish!
   Dum. O most divine Kate!
   Ber. O most profane coxcomb!   84
   Dum. By heaven, the wonder of a mortal eye!
   Ber. By earth, she is not, corporal; there you lie.
   Dum. Her amber hairs for foul have amber quoted.
   Ber. An amber-colour'd raven was well noted.   88

---

74 liver-vein: *i.e. style of a man in love (the liver being the sup-*
   posed seat of the affections)
78 All hid: *i.e. as in the game of hide and seek*
82 woodcocks: *proverbially silly birds*
87 quoted: *set down, regarded*

    Dum. As upright as the cedar.

    Ber.   Stoop, I say;

Her shoulder is with child.

    Dum.   As fair as day.

    Ber. Ay, as some days; but then no sun must shine.

    Dum. O that I had my wish!

    Long.   And I had mine! 92

    King. And [I] mine too, good Lord!

    Ber. Amen, so I had mine. Is not that a good word?

    Dum. I would forget her; but a fever she

Reigns in my blood, and will remember'd be.   96

    Ber. A fever in your blood! why, then incision

Would let her out in saucers: sweet misprision!

    Dum. Once more I'll read the ode that I have writ.

    Ber. Once more I'll mark how love can vary wit. 100

                Dumaine reads his Sonnet.

    Dum. 'On a day, alack the day!

        Love, whose month is ever May,

        Spied a blossom passing fair

        Playing in the wanton air: 104

        Through the velvet leaves the wind,

        All unseen, can passage find;

        That the lover, sick to death,

        Wish'd himself the heaven's breath.   108

        Air, quoth he, thy cheeks may blow;

        Air, would I might triumph so!

        But alack! my hand is sworn

        Ne'er to pluck thee from thy thorn: 112

        Vow, alack! for youth unmeet,

        Youth so apt to pluck a sweet.

        Do not call it sin in me,

        That I am forsworn for thee;   116

---

89 Stoop; *cf. n.*   97 incision: *blood-letting*
98 saucers: *receptacles for the blood*   misprision: *mistake*

Thou for whom e'en Jove would swear
Juno but an Ethiop were;
And deny himself for Jove,
Turning mortal for thy love.'   120

This will I send, and something else more plain,
That shall express my true love's fasting pain.
O would the King, Berowne, and Longaville
Were lovers too! Ill, to example ill,   124
Would from my forehead wipe a perjur'd note;
For none offend where all alike do dote.

   Long. [*Advancing.*] Dumaine, thy love is far from
     charity,
That in love's grief desir'st society: 128
You may look pale, but I should blush, I know,
To be o'erheard and taken napping so.

   King. [*Advancing.*] Come, sir, you blush: as his
     your case is such;
You chide at him, offending twice as much: 132
You do not love Maria; Longaville
Did never sonnet for her sake compile,
Nor never lay his wreathed arms athwart
His loving bosom to keep down his heart.   136
I have been closely shrouded in this bush,
And mark'd you both, and for you both did blush.
I heard your guilty rimes, observ'd your fashion,
Saw sighs reek from you, noted well your passion: 140
Ay me! says one; O Jove! the other cries;
One, her hairs were gold, crystal the other's eyes:
[*To Longaville.*] You would for paradise break faith
    and troth;
[*To Dumaine.*] And Jove, for your love, would in-
    fringe an oath.   144

118 Ethiop: *i.e. black as a negro*   122 fasting: *hungry, longing*
124 example: *furnish a precedent for*

What will Berowne say, when that he shall hear
Faith infringed, which such zeal did swear?
How will he scorn! how will he spend his wit!
How will he triumph, leap and laugh at it!   148
For all the wealth that ever I did see,
I would not have him know so much by me.

 Ber. Now step I forth to whip hypocrisy.
       [Descends from the tree.]

Ah! good my liege, I pray thee, pardon me: 152
Good heart! what grace hast thou, thus to reprove
These worms for loving, that art most in love?
Your eyes do make no coaches; in your tears
There is no certain princess that appears: 156
You'll not be perjur'd, 'tis a hateful thing:
Tush! none but minstrels like of sonneting.
But are you not asham'd! nay, are you not,
All three of you, to be thus much o'ershot?   160
You found his mote; the king your mote did see;
But I a beam do find in each of three.
O what a scene of foolery have I seen,
Of sighs, of groans, of sorrow, and of teen!   164
O me! with what strict patience have I sat,
To see a king transformed to a gnat;
To see great Hercules whipping a gig,
And profound Solomon to tune a jig,   168
And Nestor play at push-pin with the boys,
And critic Timon laugh at idle toys!
Where lies thy grief? O! tell me, good Dumaine.
And, gentle Longaville, where lies thy pain?   172
And where my liege's? all about the breast:

150 by: *about* 158 like of: *like* 160 o'ershot: *wide of the mark*
161 You: *i.e. Longaville* his: *i.e. Dumaine's*
164 teen: *grief, pain*   166 gnat: *a singing insect*
167 gig: *top*   168 tune: *play, or hum*
169 push-pin: *a child's game with pins*
170 critic: *cynic* toys: *trifles*

A caudle, ho!
   King.   Too bitter is thy jest.
Are we betray'd thus to thy over-view?
   Ber. Not you by me, but I betray'd to you: 176
I, that am honest; I, that hold it sin
To break the vow I am engaged in;
I am betray'd, by keeping company
With men like [men,] men of inconstancy.   180
When shall you see me write a thing in rime?
Or groan for Joan? or spend a minute's time
In pruning me? When shall you hear that I
Will praise a hand, a foot, a face, an eye,   184
A gait, a state, a brow, a breast, a waist,
A leg, a limb?—
   King.   Soft! Whither away so fast?
A true man or a thief that gallops so?
   Ber. I post from love; good lover, let me go.   188

     Enter Jaquenetta and Clown [Costard].

   Jaq. God bless the king!
   King.   What present hast thou there?
   Cost. Some certain treason.
   King.   What makes treason here?
   Cost. Nay, it makes nothing, sir.
   King.   If it mar nothing neither,
The treason and you go in peace away together.   192
   Jaq. I beseech your Grace, let this letter be read:
Our parson misdoubts it; 'twas treason, he said.
   King. Berowne, read it over.
    He [i.e. Berowne] reads the letter [in dumbshow].
Where hadst thou it?   196

174 caudle: *a warm gruel, containing wine and·spice, for the sick*
180 *Cf. n.*   183 pruning: *adorning*
185 state: *attitude, pose*   189 present: *paper to be presented*
190 makes: *does*   194 misdoubts: *suspects*

Jaq. Of Costard.

King. Where hadst thou it?

Cost. Of Dun Adramadio, Dun Adramadio.

> [*Berowne tears the letter.*]

King. How now! what is in you? why dost thou
    tear it?   200

Ber. A toy, my liege, a toy: your Grace needs not
    fear it.

Long. It did move him to passion, and therefore let's
    hear it.

Dum. [*Picking up the pieces.*] It is Berowne's
    writing, and here is his name.

Ber. [*To Costard.*] Ah, you whoreson loggerhead,
    you were born to do me shame.   204

Guilty, my lord, guilty; I confess, I confess.

King. What?

Ber. That you three fools lack'd me fool to make up
    the mess;

He, he, and you, and you my liege, and I,   208

Are pick-purses in love, and we deserve to die.

O dismiss this audience, and I shall tell you more.

Dum. Now the number is even.

Ber.   True, true; we are four.

Will these turtles be gone?

King.   Hence, sirs; away! 212

Cost. Walk aside the true folk, and let the traitors
    stay.

> [*Exeunt Costard and Jaquenetta.*]

Ber. Sweet lords, sweet lovers, O! let us embrace.

As true we are as flesh and blood can be:

The sea will ebb and flow, heaven show his face;   216

207 mess: *four persons at one table*
212 turtles: *turtle-doves, lovers*   sirs; *cf. n.*

Young blood doth not obey an old decree.

We cannot cross the cause why we were born;

Therefore, of all hands must we be forsworn.

    King. What! did these rent lines show some love of

        thine?   220

    Ber. 'Did they,' quoth you? Who sees the heavenly

        Rosaline,

That, like a rude and savage man of Inde,

    At the first opening of the gorgeous east,

Bows not his vassal head, and, strooken blind,   224

    Kisses the base ground with obedient breast?

What peremptory eagle-sighted eye

    Dares look upon the heaven of her brow,

That is not blinded by her majesty?   228

    King. What zeal, what fury, hath inspir'd thee now?

My love, her mistress, is a gracious moon;

    She, an attending star, scarce seen a light.

Ber. My eyes are then no eyes, nor I Berowne.   232

    O, but for my love, day would turn to night!

Of all complexions the cull'd sovereignty

    Do meet, as at a fair, in her fair cheek;

Where several worthies make one dignity,   236

    Where nothing wants that want itself doth seek.

Lend me the flourish of all gentle tongues,—

    Fie, painted rhetoric! O she needs it not:

To things of sale a seller's praise belongs;   240

    She passes praise; then praise too short doth blot.

A wither'd hermit, five-score winters worn,

    Might shake off fifty, looking in her eye:

218 cross . . . born: *i.e. hold out against love*
219 of all hands: *on all hands, in any case*
223 the first . . . east: *i.e. the rising of the sun*
224 strooken: *struck*   226 peremptory: *determined, bold*
236 *I.e. several beauties make one surpassing beauty*
238 flourish: *enhancement*   239 painted: *showy, artificial*

Beauty doth varnish age, as if new-born, 244
  And gives the crutch the cradle's infancy.
O 'tis the sun that maketh all things shine!
  King. By heaven, thy love is black as ebony.
Ber. Is ebony like her? O wood divine! 248
  A wife of such wood were felicity.
O who can give an oath? where is a book?
  That I may swear beauty doth beauty lack,
If that she learn not of her eye to look: 252
  No face is fair that is not full so black.
King. O paradox! Black is the badge of hell,
  The hue of dungeons and the school of night;
And beauty's crest becomes the heavens well. 256
  Ber. Devils soonest tempt, resembling spirits of light.
O, if in black my lady's brows be deck'd,
  It mourns that painting [and] usurping hair
Should ravish doters with a false aspect; 260
  And therefore is she born to make black fair.
Her favour turns the fashion of the days,
  For native blood is counted painting now;
And therefore red, that would avoid dispraise, 264
  Paints itself black, to imitate her brow.
Dum. To look like her are chimney-sweepers black.
  Long. And since her time are colliers counted bright.
King. And Ethiops of their sweet complexion crack. 268
  Dum. Dark needs no candles now, for dark is light.
Ber. Your mistresses dare never come in rain,
  For fear their colours should be wash'd away.

255 school of night; *cf. n.*   256 *Cf. n.*
257 resembling: *taking the form of; cf. n.*   259 usurping: *false*
262 favour: *face*   267 counted: *accounted*
268 crack: *boast*

King. 'Twere good yours did; for, sir, to tell you
    plain,   272
    I'll find a fairer face not wash'd to-day.
Ber. I'll prove her fair, or talk till doomsday here.
   King. No devil will fright thee then so much as she.
Dum. I never knew man hold vile stuff so dear.   276
   Long. Look, here's thy love: [*Showing his shoe.*]
    my foot and her face see.
Ber. O, if the streets were paved with thine eyes,
    Her feet were much too dainty for such tread.
Dum. O vile! then, as she goes, what upward lies   280
    The street should see as she walk'd overhead.
King. But what of this? Are we not all in love?
   Ber. Nothing so sure; and thereby all forsworn.
King. Then leave this chat; and good Berowne, now
    prove   284
    Our loving lawful, and our faith not torn.
Dum. Ay, marry, there; some flattery for this evil.
   Long. O some authority how to proceed;
Some tricks, some quillets, how to cheat the devil.   288
   Dum. Some salve for perjury.
   Ber.   O, 'tis more than need.
Have at you, then, affection's men at-arms!
Consider what you first did swear unto:
To fast, to study, and to see no woman;   292
Flat treason 'gainst the kingly state of youth.
Say, can you fast? your stomachs are too young,
And abstinence engenders maladies.
And where that you have vow'd to study, lords,   296
In that each of you hath forsworn his book,
Can you still dream and pore and thereon look?

275 then: *i.e. at doomsday*   288 quillets: *quibbles*
290 affection's: *love's*
297 In that: *in as much as*   book: *true book, i.e. woman's face*
   or eyes; cf. line 319*

For when would you, my lord, or you, or you,
Have found the ground of study's excellence   300
Without the beauty of a woman's face?
From women's eyes this doctrine I derive:
They are the ground, the books, the academes,
From whence doth spring the true Promethean fire. 304
Why, universal plodding poisons up
The nimble spirits in the arteries,
As motion and long-during action tires
The sinewy vigour of the traveller.   308
Now, for not looking on a woman's face,
You have in that forsworn the use of eyes,
And study too, the causer of your vow;
For where is any author in the world   312
Teaches such beauty as a woman's eye?
Learning is but an adjunct to ourself,
And where we are our learning likewise is:
Then when ourselves we see in ladies' eyes,   316
Do we not likewise see our learning there?
O we have made a vow to study, lords,
And in that vow we have forsworn our books:
For when would you, my liege, or you, or you,   320
In leaden contemplation have found out
Such fiery numbers as the prompting eyes
Of beauty's tutors have enrich'd you with?
Other slow arts entirely keep the brain,   324
And therefore, finding barren practisers,
Scarce show a harvest of their heavy toil;
But love, first learned in a lady's eyes,
Lives not alone immured in the brain,   328
But, with the motion of all elements,

299-304 *Cf. n.*   304 Promethean: *divine*
305 poisons up; *cf. n.*   306 arteries; *cf. n.*
321 leaden: *heavy, dull*   322 numbers: *verses, poems*
324 keep: *remain in*

Courses as swift as thought in every power,
And gives to every power a double power,
Above their functions and their offices.   332
It adds a precious seeing to the eye:
A lover's eyes will gaze an eagle blind;
A lover's ear will hear the lowest sound,
When the suspicious head of theft is stopp'd: 336
Love's feeling is more soft and sensible
Than are the tender horns of cockled snails:
Love's tongue proves dainty Bacchus gross in taste.
For valour, is not Love a Hercules,   340
Still climbing trees in the Hesperides?
Subtle as Sphinx; as sweet and musical
As bright Apollo's lute, strung with his hair;
And when Love speaks, the voice of all the gods   344
Make heaven drowsy with the harmony.
Never durst poet touch a pen to write
Until his ink were temper'd with Love's sighs;
O! then his lines would ravish savage ears,   348
And plant in tyrants mild humility.
From women's eyes this doctrine I derive:
They sparkle still the right Promethean fire;
They are the books, the arts, the academes,   352
That show, contain, and nourish all the world;
Else none at all in aught proves excellent.
Then fools you were these women to forswear,
Or, keeping what is sworn, you will prove fools.   356
For wisdom's sake, a word that all men love,
Or for love's sake, a word that loves all men,
Or for men's sake, the authors of these women;
Or women's sake, by whom we men are men,   360
Let us once lose our oaths to find ourselves,

336 *Cf. n.*   338 cockled: *inclosed in a shell*
341 Hesperides: *i.e. the garden of the Hesperides*
344 voice: *i.e. responsive voice*   358 loves: *cherishes, benefits*

Or else we lose ourselves to keep our oaths.
It is religion to be thus forsworn;
For charity itself fulfils the law;   364
And who can sever love from charity?

King. Saint Cupid, then! and, soldiers, to the field!

Ber. Advance your standards, and upon them, lords!
Pell-mell, down with them! but be first advis'd,   368
In conflict that you get the sun of them.

Long. Now to plain-dealing; lay these glozes by:
Shall we resolve to woo these girls of France?

King. And win them too: therefore let us devise 372
Some entertainment for them in their tents.

Ber. First, from the park let us conduct them
        thither;
Then homeward every man attach the hand
Of his fair mistress: in the afternoon   376
We will with some strange pastime solace them,
Such as the shortness of the time can shape;
For revels, dances, masks, and merry hours
Forerun fair Love, strewing her way with flowers. 380

King. Away, away! no time shall be omitted,
That will betime, and may by us be fitted.

Ber. Allons! allons! Sow'd cockle reap'd no corn;
        And justice always whirls in equal measure: 384
Light wenches may prove plagues to men forsworn;
        If so, our copper buys no better treasure.

                                                    Exeunt.

364 *Cf. n.*   369 sun: *advantage of position*
370 glozes: *sophistries*   382 betime: *betide, chance*
383 Sow'd cockle; *cf. n.*   386 copper: *base coin*

ACT FIFTH

Scene One

[*The King of Navarre's Park*]

*Enter the Pedant [Holofernes], the Curate
[Nathaniel], and Dull.*

Hol. Satis quod sufficit.

Nath. I praise God for you, sir: your reasons
at dinner have been sharp and sententious;
pleasant without scurrility, witty without affec- 4
tion, audacious without impudency, learned
without opinion, and strange without heresy. I
did converse this quondam day with a com-
panion of the king's, who is intituled, nomi- 8
nated, or called, Don Adriano de Armado.

Hol. Novi hominem tanquam te: his humour
is lofty, his discourse peremptory, his tongue
filed, his eye ambitious, his gait majestical, and 12
his general behaviour vain, ridiculous, and
thrasonical. He is too picked, too spruce, too
affected, too odd, as it were, too peregrinate, as
I may call it. 16

Nath. A most singular and choice epithet.

                   Draw out his table-book.

Hol. He draweth out the thread of his verbo-
sity finer than the staple of his argument. I
abhor such fanatical phantasimes, such insoci- 20

---

1 Satis quod sufficit: *Enough is as good as a feast*
2 reasons: *arguments, discourse*   . 4 affection: *affectation*
6 opinion: *self-conceit*   strange: *novel, original*
10 Novi . . . te: *I know the man as well as I know you*
12 filed: *polished*
14 thrasonical: *boastful*   picked: *fastidious*
15 peregrinate: *traveled, foreign*   19 staple: *fiber*

able and point-devise companions; such rackers
of orthography, as to speak 'dout,' fine, when he
should say 'doubt'; 'det,' when he should pronounce 'debt,'—d, e, b, t, not d, e, t: he clepeth a 24
calf, cauf; half, hauf; neighbour *vocatur* nebour,
neigh abbreviated ne. This is abhominable,
which he would call abominable,—it insinuateth
me of insanie: *ne intelligis, domine?* To 28
make frantic, lunatic.

Nath. Laus Deo bene intelligo.

Hol. Bon, bon, fort bon! Priscian a little
scratched; 'twill serve. 32

Enter Braggart [*Armado*], Boy [*Moth,
and Costard*].

Nath. Videsne quis venit?

Hol. Video, et gaudeo.

Arm. [*To Moth.*] Chirrah!

Hol. Quare chirrah, not sirrah? 36

Arm. Men of peace, well encountered.

Hol. Most military sir, salutation.

Moth. [*Aside to Costard.*] They have been
at a great feast of languages, and stolen the 40
scraps.

Cost. O! they have lived long on the alms-
basket of words. I marvel thy master hath not
eaten thee for a word; for thou art not so long 44
by the head as *honorificabilitudinitatibus:* thou
art easier swallowed than a flap-dragon.

Moth. Peace! the peal begins.

21 point-devise: *precise*   22 fine: *mincingly; cf. n.*
24 clepeth: *calls*   25 vocatur: *is called, pronounced*
28 insanie: *insanity*   ne . . . domine: *do you understand, sir?*
30 Laus . . . intelligo: *God be praised, I understand well*
31 Priscian; *cf. n.*   33 Videsne . . . venit: *Do you see who comes?*
34 Video, et gaudeo: *I see and am pleased*   36 Quare: *why*
45 honorifi- etc.; *cf. n.*   46 flap-dragon: *a raisin set on fire in brandy*

Arm. [*To Holofernes.*] Monsieur, are you 48
not lettered?

Moth. Yes, yes; he teaches boys the horn-
book. What is a, b, spelt backward, with the
horn on his head?   52

Hol. Ba, *pueritia*, with a horn added.

Moth. Ba! most silly sheep with a horn. You
hear his learning.

Hol. Quis, quis, thou consonant?   56

Moth. The third of the five vowels, if you
repeat them; or the fifth, if I.

Hol. I will repeat them,—a, e, i,—

Moth. The sheep; the other two concludes 60
it,—o, u.

Arm. Now, by the salt wave of the Mediter-
raneum, a sweet touch, a quick venew of wit!
snip, snap, quick and home! it rejoiceth my 64
intellect: true wit!

Moth. Offered by a child to an old man;
which is wit-old.

Hol. What is the figure? what is the figure? 68

Moth. Horns.

Hol. Thou disputest like an infant; go, whip
thy gig.

Moth. Lend me your horn to make one, and 72
I will whip about your infamy *circum circa*. A
gig of a cuckold's horn.

Cost. An I had but one penny in the world,
thou shouldst have it to buy gingerbread. Hold, 76
there is the very remuneration I had of thy
master, thou halfpenny purse of wit, thou

50 horn-book: *primer; cf. n.*   53 pueritia: *childishness, child*
61 o, u: *i.e. oh, you*   63 venew: *venue, sally*
67 wit-old: *i.e. wittol, cuckold*
73 circum circa: *round and round; cf. n.*

pigeon-egg of discretion. O, an the heavens were
so pleased that thou wert but my bastard, what 80
a joyful father wouldst thou make me! Go to;
thou hast it *ad dunghill,* at the fingers' ends, as
they say.

Hol. O! I smell false Latin! dunghill for 84
unguem.

Arm. Arts-man, *præambula:* we will be
singled from the barbarous. Do you not educate
youth at the charge-house on the top of the 88
mountain?

Hol. Or *mons,* the hill.

Arm. At your sweet pleasure, for the mountain.   92

Hol. I do, sans question.

Arm. Sir, it is the king's most sweet pleasure
and affection to congratulate the princess at her
pavilion in the posteriors of this day, which the 96
rude multitude call the afternoon.

Hol. The posterior of the day, most generous sir, is liable, congruent, and measurable
for the afternoon: the word is well culled, 100
chose, sweet and apt, I do assure you, sir; I do
assure.

Arm. Sir, the king is a noble gentleman, and
my familiar, I do assure ye, very good friend. 104
For what is inward between us, let it pass: I do
beseech thee, remember thy courtesy; I beseech
thee, apparel thy head: and among other im-
portunate and most serious designs, and of great 108
import indeed, too, but let that pass: for I must

82 ad dunghill; *cf. n.*
86 Arts-man: *professor of the liberal arts*   præambula: *come*
    forward   88 charge-house: *schoolhouse; cf. n.*
98 generous: *well-born*   99 liable: *suitable*
'05 inward: *private*   106 remember . . . courtesy: *put on your hat*

tell thee, it will please his Grace, by the world,
sometime to lean upon my poor shoulder, and
with his royal finger, thus dally with my excre- 112
ment, with my mustachio: but, sweet heart, let
that pass. By the world, I recount no fable:
some certain special honours it pleaseth his
greatness to impart to Armado, a soldier, a man 116
of travel, that hath seen the world: but let that
pass. The very all of all is, but, sweet heart, I do
implore secrecy, that the king would have me
present the princess, sweet chuck, with some 120
delightful ostentation, or show, or pageant, or
antick, or fire-work. Now, understanding that
the curate and your sweet self are good at such
eruptions and sudden breaking out of mirth, as 124
it were, I have acquainted you withal, to the end
to crave your assistance.

Hol. Sir, you shall present before her the
Nine Worthies. Sir Nathaniel, as concerning 128
some entertainment of time, some show in the
posterior of this day, to be rendered by our
assistants, the king's command, and this
most gallant, illustrate, and learned gentleman, 132
before the princess; I say, none so fit as to present the Nine Worthies.

Nath. Where will you find men worthy
enough to present them?   136

Hol. Joshua, yourself; myself, or this gallant
gentleman, Judas Maccabæus; this swain, because of his great limb, or joint, shall pass
Pompey the Great; the page, Hercules,—   140

Arm. Pardon, sir; error: he is not quantity

112 excrement: *excrescence, hair on lip*   120 chuck: *a pet name*
128 Nine Worthies; *cf. n.*   139 pass: *pass for* (?), *surpass* (?)

enough for that Worthy's thumb: he is not so
big as the end of his club.

Hol. Shall I have audience? he shall present 144
Hercules in minority: his enter and exit shall be
strangling a snake; and I will have an apology
for that purpose.

Moth. An excellent device! so, if any of 148
the audience hiss, you may cry, 'Well done,
Hercules! now thou crushest the snake!' that is
the way to make an offence gracious, though
few have the grace to do it.   152

Arm. For the rest of the Worthies?—

Hol. I will play three myself.

Moth. Thrice-worthy gentleman!

Arm. Shall I tell you a thing?   156

Hol. We attend.

Arm. We will have, if this fadge not, an
antick. I beseech you, follow.

Hol. Via, goodman Dull! thou hast spoken 160
no word all this while.

Dull. Nor understood none neither, sir.

Hol. Allons! we will employ thee.

Dull. I'll make one in a dance, or so; or I 164
will play on the tabor to the Worthies, and let them
dance the hay.

Hol. Most dull, honest Dull, to our sport,
away!   *Exeunt.*

145 Hercules in minority; *cf. n.*   158 fadge: *succeed*
159 antick: *grotesque entertainment*   160 Via: *On your way!*
165 tabor: *a small drum*

Scene Two

[*The same.   Before the Princess's Pavilion*]

Enter the Ladies [*i.e. Princess, Katharine,
Rosaline, and Maria*].

Prin. Sweet hearts, we shall be rich ere we depart,
If fairings come thus plentifully in.
A lady wall'd about with diamonds!
Look you what I have from the loving king.   4
   Ros. Madam, came nothing else along with that?
   Prin. Nothing but this! yes, as much love in rime
As would be cramm'd up in a sheet of paper,
Writ o' both sides the leaf, margent and all,   8
That he was fain to seal on Cupid's name.
   Ros. That was the way to make his godhead wax;
For he hath been five thousand year a boy.
   Kath. Ay, and a shrewd unhappy gallows too.   12
   Ros. You'll ne'er be friends with him: a' kill'd your
      sister.
   Kath. He made her melancholy, sad, and heavy;
And so she died: had she been light, like you,
Of such a merry, nimble, stirring spirit,   16
She might ha' been a grandam ere she died;
And so may you, for a light heart lives long.
   Ros. What's your dark meaning, mouse, of this light
      word?
   Kath. A light condition in a beauty dark.   20
   Ros. We need more light to find your meaning out.
   Kath. You'll mar the light by taking it in snuff;

166 hay: *country dance*
2 fairings: *presents, originally such as were bought at a fair*
9 That: *so that (there being no blank space left)*
10 wax: *grow (with quibble on sealing-wax)*
12 shrewd . . . gallows: *cunning, roguish knave*
13 *Cf. n.*   20 condition: *temperament*
22 in snuff: *in anger, ill (with pun on the snuff of a candle)*

Therefore, I'll darkly end the argument.

    Ros. Look, what you do, you do it still i' the dark. 24

    Kath. So do not you, for you are a light wench.

    Ros. Indeed I weigh not you, and therefore light.

    Kath. You weigh me not. O! that's you care not for me.

    Ros. Great reason; for, 'past cure is still past care.'   28

    Prin. Well bandied both; a set of wit well play'd.
But Rosaline, you have a favour too:
Who sent it? and what is it?

    Ros.   I would you knew:
An if my face were but as fair as yours,   32
My favour were as great; be witness this.
Nay, I have verses too, I thank Berowne:
The numbers true; and, were the numb'ring too,
I were the fairest goddess on the ground: 36
I am compar'd to twenty thousand fairs.
O, he hath drawn my picture in his letter!

    Prin. Anything like?

    Ros. Much in the letters, nothing in the praise.   40

    Prin. Beauteous as ink; a good conclusion.

    Kath. Fair as a text B in a copy-book.

    Ros. 'Ware pencils, ho! let me not die your debtor,
My red dominical, my golden letter: 44
O, that your face were not so full of O's!

    Prin. A pox of that jest! and I beshrew all shrows!
But, Katharine, what was sent to you from fair Dumaine?

    Kath. Madam, this glove.

    Prin.   Did he not send you twain? 48

26 weigh; *cf. n.*
35 numbers: *rhythm*   numb'ring: *estimate*
30 favour: *gift; also face*
40 letters; *cf. n.*
43 'Ware pencils; *cf. n.*
45 O's: *marks left by the smallpox*
42 text B; *cf. n.*
44 red dominical; *cf. n.*
46 shrows: *shrews*

Kath. Yes, madam; and moreover,
Some thousand verses of a faithful lover:
A huge translation of hypocrisy,
Vilely compil'd, profound simplicity.   52
    Mar. This, and these pearls to me sent Longaville:
The letter is too long by half a mile.
    Prin. I think no less. Dost thou not wish in heart
The chain were longer and the letter short?   56
    Mar. Ay, or I would these hands might never part.
    Prin. We are wise girls to mock our lovers so.
    Ros. They are worse fools to purchase mocking so.
That same Berowne I'll torture ere I go.   60
O that I knew he were but in by the week!
How I would make him fawn, and beg, and seek,
And wait the season, and observe the times,
And spend his prodigal wits in bootless rimes,   64
And shape his service wholly to my hests,
And make him proud to make me proud that jests!
So perttaunt-like would I o'ersway his state
That he should be my fool, and I his fate.   68
    Prin. None are so surely caught, when they are
        catch'd,
As wit turn'd fool. folly, in wisdom hatch'd,
Hath wisdom's warrant and the help of school
And wit's own grace to grace a learned fool.   72
    Ros. The blood of youth burns not with such excess
As gravity's revolt to wantonness.
    Mar. Folly in fools bears not so strong a note
As foolery in the wise, when wit doth dote;   76
Since all the power thereof it doth apply
To prove, by wit, worth in simplicity.

Enter Boyet.

51 translation of hypocrisy; *cf. n.*   61 in . . . week; *cf. n.*
65 hests: *behests; cf. n.*   67 perttaunt-like; *cf. n.*

    Prin. Here comes Boyet, and mirth is in his face.

    Boyet. O, I am stabb'd with laughter! Where's her
      Grace?   80

    Prin. Thy news, Boyet?

    Boyet.   Prepare, madam, prepare!—
Arm, wenches, arm! encounters mounted are
Against your peace: Love doth approach disguis'd,
Armed in arguments; you'll be surpris'd: 84
Muster your wits; stand in your own defence;
Or hide your heads like cowards, and fly hence.

    Prin. Saint Denis to Saint Cupid! What are they
That charge their breath against us? say, scout, say. 88

    Boyet. Under the cool shade of a sycamore
I thought to close mine eyes some half an hour,
When, lo! to interrupt my purpos'd rest,
Toward that shade I might behold addrest   92
The king and his companions: warily
I stole into a neighbour thicket by,
And overheard what you shall overhear;
That, by and by, disguis'd they will be here.   96
Their herald is a pretty knavish page,
That well by heart hath conn'd his embassage:
Action and accent did they teach him there;
'Thus must thou speak, and thus thy body bear.'   100
And ever and anon they made a doubt
Presence majestical would put him out;
'For,' quoth the king, 'an angel shalt thou see;
Yet fear not thou, but speak audaciously.'   104
The boy replied, 'An angel is not evil;
I should have fear'd her had she been a devil.'
With that all laugh'd and clapp'd him on the shoulder,
Making the bold wag by their praises bolder.   108

82 encounters: *assailants*   87 Saint Denis: *patron saint of France*
92 addrest: *coming straight*   96 by and by: *soon*
101 made a doubt: *expressed fear*   104 audaciously: *boldly*

One rubb'd his elbow thus, and fleer'd, and swore
A better speech was never spoke before;
Another, with his finger and his thumb,
Cry'd 'Via! we will do 't, come what will come';   112
The third he caper'd and cried, 'All goes well';
The fourth turn'd on the toe, and down he fell.
With that, they all did tumble on the ground,
With such a zealous laughter, so profound,   116
That in this spleen ridiculous appears,
To check their folly, passion's solemn tears.

 Prin. But what, but what? come they to visit us?

 Boyet. They do, they do; and are apparell'd
  thus,   120
Like Muscovites or Russians, as I guess.
Their purpose is to parle, to court and dance;
And every one his love-feat will advance
Unto his several mistress, which they'll know   124
By favours several which they did bestow.

 Prin. And will they so? the gallants shall be task'd:
For, ladies, we will every one be mask'd,
And not a man of them shall have the grace,   128
Despite of suit, to see a lady's face.
Hold, Rosaline, this favour thou shalt wear,
And then the king will court thee for his dear:
Hold, take thou this, my sweet, and give me thine, 132
So shall Berowne take me for Rosaline,
And change you favours too; so shall your loves
Woo contrary, deceiv'd by these removes.

 Ros. Come on, then; wear the favours most in
  sight.   136

 Kath. But in this changing what is your intent?

 Prin. The effect of my intent is, to cross theirs:

109 fleer'd: *grinned*   117 spleen ridiculous: *ridiculous merriment*
118 solemn: *sober*   121 Like Muscovites; *cf. n.*
126 task'd: *given a task or problem*   135 removes: *exchanges*

They do it but in mockery merriment;
And mock for mock is only my intent.   140
Their several counsels they unbosom shall
To loves mistook and so be mock'd withal
Upon the next occasion that we meet,
With visages display'd, to talk and greet.   144

    Ros. But shall we dance, if they desire us to 't?

    Prin. No, to the death, we will not move a foot:
Nor to their penn'd speech render we no grace;
But while 'tis spoke each turn away her face.   148

    Boyet. Why, that contempt will kill the speaker's heart,
And quite divorce his memory from his part.

    Prin. Therefore I do it; and I make no doubt,
The rest will ne'er come in, if he be out.   152
There's no such sport as sport by sport o'erthrown,
To make theirs ours and ours none but our own:
So shall we stay, mocking intended game,
And they, well mock'd, depart away with shame.   156
                                     Sound Trumpets.

    Boyet. The trumpet sounds: be mask'd; the maskers
    come.   *[The Ladies mask.]*

*Enter Blackamoors with music; the Boy [Moth] with
    a speech, and the rest of the Lords disguised.*

    Moth. 'All hail, the richest beauties on the earth!'

    Boyet. Beauties no richer than rich taffeta.

    Moth. 'A holy parcel of the fairest dames,   160
             The Ladies turn their backs to him.
That ever turn'd their—backs—to mortal views!'

    Ber. 'Their eyes,' villain, 'their eyes.'

    Moth. 'That ever turn'd their eyes to mortal views!
Out—'   164

154 theirs: *their sport*   155 intended game: *the jest they intend*
159 taffeta: *i.e. the taffeta, or silk, masks*

Boyet. True; 'out,' indeed.

Moth. 'Out of your favours, heavenly spirits, vouchsafe
Not to behold'—

    Ber. 'Once to behold,' rogue.   168

Moth. 'Once to behold with your sun-beamed eyes,
—with your sun-beamed eyes'—

Boyet. They will not answer to that epithet;
You were best call it 'daughter-beamed eyes.'   172

Moth. They do not mark me, and that brings me out.

Ber. Is this your perfectness? be gone, you rogue!

                      [Exit Moth.]

Ros. What would these strangers? know their minds,
   Boyet:
If they do speak our language, 'tis our will   176
That some plain man recount their purposes:
Know what they would.

Boyet. What would you with the princess?

Ber. Nothing but peace and gentle visitation.   180

Ros. What would they, say they?

Boyet. Nothing but peace and gentle visitation.

Ros. Why, that they have; and bid them so be gone.

Boyet. She says, you have it, and you may be
   gone.   184

King. Say to her, we have measur'd many miles,
To tread a measure with her on this grass.

Boyet. They say that they have measur'd many a
   mile,
To tread a measure with you on this grass.   188

Ros. It is not so. Ask them how many inches
Is in one mile: if they have measur'd many,
The measure then of one is easily told.

186 measure: *stately dance*

Boyet. If to come hither you have measur'd
    miles,   192
And many miles, the princess bids you tell
How many inches do fill up one mile.
    Ber. Tell her we measure them by weary steps.
    Boyet. She hears herself.
    Ros.   How many weary steps, 196
Of many weary miles you have o'ergone,
Are number'd in the travel of one mile?
    Ber. We number nothing that we spend for you:
Our duty is so rich, so infinite,   200
That we may do it still without accompt.
Vouchsafe to show the sunshine of your face,
That we, like savages, may worship it.
    Ros. My face is but a moon, and clouded too.   204
    King. Blessed are clouds, to do as such clouds do!
Vouchsafe, bright moon, and these thy stars, to shine,
Those clouds remov'd, upon our wat'ry eyne.
    Ros. O vain petitioner! beg a greater matter;   208
Thou now requests but moonshine in the water.
    King. Then, in our measure vouchsafe but one
    change.
Thou bid'st me beg; this begging is not strange.
    Ros. Play, music, then! Nay, you must do it soon. 212
                             [*Music plays.*]
Not yet! no dance! thus change I like the moon.
    King. Will you not dance? How come you thus
    estrang'd?
    Ros. You took the moon at full, but now she's
    chang'd.
    King. Yet still she is the moon, and I the man.   216
The music plays; vouchsafe some motion to it.

201 accompt: *reckoning*   207 eyne: *eyes*
209 requests: *requestest*   210 change: *round or 'figure' in dancing*
216 man: *i.e. man in the moon*

Ros. Our ears vouchsafe it.

King.   But your legs should do it.

Ros. Since you are strangers, and come here by
  chance,
We'll not be nice: take hands: we will not dance.   220

King. Why take we hands then?

Ros.   Only to part friends.
Curtsy, sweet hearts; and so the measure ends.

King. More measure of this measure: be not nice.

Ros. We can afford no more at such a price.   224

King. Prize you yourselves. What buys your company?

Ros. Your absence only.

King.   That can never be.

Ros. Then cannot we be bought: and so, adieu;
Twice to your visor, and half once to you!   228

King. If you deny to dance, let's hold more chat.

Ros. In private, then.

King.   I am best pleas'd with that.
                    [*They converse apart.*]

Ber. White-handed mistress, one sweet word with
  thee.

Prin. Honey, and milk, and sugar; there are
  three.   232

Ber. Nay then, two treys, an if you grow so nice,
Metheglin, wort, and malmsey: well run, dice!
There's half a dozen sweets.

Prin.   Seventh sweet, adieu:
Since you can cog, I'll play no more with you.   236

Ber. One word in secret.

225 Prize: *set a price on*   228 Twice: *i.e. twice adieu*
233 treys: *threes*
234 Metheglin: *mead containing honey*
  beer   malmsey: *a sweet wine*   wort: *sweet unfermented*
                                                  236 cog: *cheat*

Prin.   Let it not be sweet.

Ber. Thou griev'st my gall.

Prin.   Gall! bitter.

Ber.   Therefore meet.

                                  [*They converse apart.*]

Dum. Will you vouchsafe with me to change a word?

Mar. Name it.

Dum.   Fair lady,—

Mar.   Say you so? Fair lord! 240
Take that for your 'fair lady.'

Dum.   Please it you,
As much in private, and I'll bid adieu.

                                  [*They converse apart.*]

Kath. What! was your vizard made without a tongue?

Long. I know the reason, lady, why you ask.   244

Kath. O for your reason; quickly, sir; I long.

Long. You have a double tongue within your mask,
And would afford my speechless vizard half.

Kath. 'Veal,' quoth the Dutchman. Is not 'veal' a calf?   248

Long. A calf, fair lady!

Kath.   No, a fair lord calf.

Long. Let's part the word.

Kath.   No, I'll not be your half:
Take all, and wean it: it may prove an ox.

Long. Look, how you butt yourself in these sharp mocks.   252
Will you give horns, chaste lady? do not so.

Kath. Then die a calf, before your horns do grow.

Long. One word in private with you, ere I die.

 Kath. Bleat softly then; the butcher hears you
  cry.   256
           [They converse apart.]
Boyet. The tongues of mocking wenches are as keen
 As is the razor's edge invisible,
Cutting a smaller hair than may be seen,
 Above the sense of sense; so sensible 260
Seemeth their conference; their conceits have wings
Fleeter than arrows, bullets, wind, thought, swifter
  things.
 Ros. Not one word more, my maids: break off,
  break off.
 Ber. By heaven, all dry-beaten with pure scoff! 264
 King. Farewell, mad wenches: you have simple wits.
         Exeunt [King and Lords].
 Prin. Twenty adieus, my frozen Muscovits.
Are these the breed of wits so wonder'd at?
 Boyet. Tapers they are, with your sweet breaths
  puff'd out.   268
Ros. Well-liking wits they have; gross, gross; fat, fat.
 Prin. O poverty in wit, kingly-poor flout!
Will they not, think you, hang themselves to-night?
 Or ever, but in vizards, show their faces? 272
This pert Berowne was out of countenance quite.
 Ros. They were all in lamentable cases.
The king was weeping-ripe for a good word.
 Prin. Berowne did swear himself out of all suit. 276
Mar. Dumaine was at my service, and his sword:
 'No point,' quoth I: my servant straight was mute.
Kath. Lord Longaville said, I came o'er his heart;

---

260 sense of sense: *i.e. perception* sensible: *sensitive*
261 conference: *conversation* conceits: *fancies*
264 dry-beaten: *cudgeled*   269 Well-liking: *plump*
270 kingly-poor flout: *a fling poor for a king*
275 weeping-ripe for: *ready to weep for want of*
278 No point; *cf. II. i.* 188

And trow you what he call'd me?

Prin.   Qualm, perhaps. 280

Kath. Yes, in good faith.

Prin.   Go, sickness as thou art!

Ros. Well, better wits have worn plain statute-caps.
But will you hear? the king is my love sworn.

Prin. And quick Berowne hath plighted faith to
me.   284

Kath. And Longaville was for my service born.

Mar. Dumaine is mine, as sure as bark on tree.

Boyet. Madam, and pretty mistresses, give ear:
Immediately they will again be here   288
In their own shapes; for it can never be
They will digest this harsh indignity.

Prin. Will they return?

Boyet.   They will, they will, God knows;
And leap for joy, though they are lame with blows: 292
Therefore change favours; and, when they repair,
Blow like sweet roses in this summer air.

Prin. How blow? how blow? speak to be understood.

Boyet. Fair ladies, mask'd, are roses in their bud: 296
Dismask'd, their damask sweet commixture shown,
Are angels vailing clouds, or roses blown.

Prin. Avaunt, perplexity! What shall we do,
If they return in their own shapes to woo?   300

Ros. Good madam, if by me you'll be advis'd,
Let's mock them still, as well known as disguis'd.
Let us complain to them what fools were here,
Disguis'd like Muscovites, in shapeless gear;   304
And wonder what they were, and to what end
Their shallow shows and prologue vilely penn'd,
And their rough carriage so ridiculous,

280 Qualm: *calm; cf. n.*   282 statute-caps: *woollen caps; cf. n.*
290 digest: *put up with, 'swallow'*   297 commixture: *complexion*
298 vailing: *letting fal'*   blown: *full blown*

Should be presented at our tent to us.   308
   Boyet. Ladies, withdraw: the gallants are at hand.
   Prin. Whip to your tents, as roes runs o'er land.
        Exeunt [Princess, Ros., Kath., and Maria].

   Enter the King and the rest [of the Lords].

   King. Fair sir, God save you! Where is the prin-
cess?
   Boyet. Gone to her tent. Please it your majesty, 312
Command me any service to her thither?
   King. That she vouchsafe me audience for one word.
   Boyet. I will; and so will she, I know, my lord.
        Exit.

   Ber. This fellow pecks up wit, as pigeons pease, 316
And utters it again when God doth please:
He is wit's pedlar, and retails his wares
At wakes and wassails, meetings, markets, fairs;
And we that sell by gross, the Lord doth know,   320
Have not the grace to grace it with such show.
This gallant pins the wenches on his sleeve;
Had he been Adam, he had tempted Eve:
He can carve too, and lisp: why, this is he   324
That kiss'd his hand away in courtesy.
This is the ape of form, monsieur the nice,
That, when he plays at tables, chides the dice
In honourable terms: nay, he can sing   328
A mean most meanly, and in ushering
Mend him who can: the ladies call him sweet;
The stairs, as he treads on them, kiss his feet.
This is the flower that smiles on every one,   332
To show his teeth as white as whales-bone;

310 runs: *run*
319 wakes: *night festivals*   wassails: *drinking bouts*
324 can carve: *knows the art of amorous glance and gesture*
327 tables: *backgammon*   329 mean: *tenor*
333 whales-bone: *whale's bone, walrus tusk*

And consciences, that will not die in debt,
Pay him the due of honey-tongu'd Boyet.
> *King.* A blister on his sweet tongue, with my
> heart,   336
That put Armado's page out of his part!

Enter the Ladies [with Boyet].

> *Ber.* See where it comes! Behaviour, what wert
> thou,
Till this man show'd thee? and what art thou now?
King. All hail, sweet madam, and fair time of day! 340
> *Prin.* 'Fair,' in 'all hail,' is foul, as I conceive.
King. Construe my speeches better, if you may.
> *Prin.* Then wish me better: I will give you leave.
King. We came to visit you, and purpose now   344
> To lead you to our court: vouchsafe it then.
Prin. This field shall hold me, and so hold your vow:
> Nor God, nor I, delights in perjur'd men.
King. Rebuke me not for that which you provoke: 348
> The virtue of your eye must break my oath.
Prin. You nickname virtue; vice you should have
> spoke;
For virtue's office never breaks men's troth.
Now, by my maiden honour, yet as pure   352
> As the unsullied lily, I protest,
A world of torments though I should endure,
> I would not yield to be your house's guest;
So much I hate a breaking cause to be   356
Of heavenly oaths, vow'd with integrity.
King. O, you have liv'd in desolation here,
> Unseen, unvisited, much to our shame.
Prin. Not so, my lord; it is not so, I swear;   360
> We have had pastimes here and pleasant game.

339 man; *cf. n.*   350 nickname: *misname*

A mess of Russians left us but of late.
    King. How, madam! Russians?
    Prin.   Ay, in truth, my lord;
Trim gallants, full of courtship and of state.   364
    Ros. Madam, speak true. It is not so, my lord:
My lady, to the manner of the days,
In courtesy gives undeserving praise.
We four, indeed, confronted were with four   368
In Russian habit: here they stay'd an hour,
And talk'd apace; and in that hour, my lord,
They did not bless us with one happy word.
I dare not call them fools; but this I think,   372
When they are thirsty, fools would fain have drink.
    Ber. This jest is dry to me. Gentle sweet,
Your wit makes wise things foolish: when we greet,
With eyes best seeing, heaven's fiery eye,   376
By light we lose light: your capacity
Is of that nature that to your huge store
Wise things seem foolish and rich things but poor.
    Ros. This proves you wise and rich, for in my
      eye—   380
    Ber. I am a fool, and full of poverty.
    Ros. But that you take what doth to you belong,
It were a fault to snatch words from my tongue.
    Ber. O, I am yours, and all that I possess.   384
    Ros. All the fool mine?
    Ber.   I cannot give you less.
    Ros. Which of the vizards was it that you wore?
    Ber. Where? when? what vizard? why demand you
      this?
    Ros. There, then, that vizard; that superfluous
      case   388

362 mess; *cf. IV. iii.* 207   366 to the manner: *after the fashion*
374 dry: *without savor* (*with pun on 'thirsty'*)

That hid the worse, and show'd the better face.

    King. We were descried: they'll mock us now down-
       right.

    Dum. Let us confess, and turn it to a jest.

    Prin. Amaz'd, my lord?   Why looks your highness
      sad?   392

    Ros. Help! hold his brows! he'll sound.   Why look
      you pale?

Sea-sick, I think, coming from Muscovy.

Ber. Thus pour the stars down plagues for perjury.

    Can any face of brass hold longer out?—   396

Here stand I, lady; dart thy skill at me;

    Bruise me with scorn, confound me with a flout;

Thrust thy sharp wit quite through my ignorance;

    Cut me to pieces with thy keen conceit;   400

And I will wish thee never more to dance,

    Nor never more in Russian habit wait.

O, never will I trust to speeches penn'd,

    Nor to the motion of a schoolboy's tongue,   404

Nor never come in vizard to my friend,

    Nor woo in rime, like a blind harper's song.

Taffeta phrases, silken terms precise,

    Three-pil'd hyperboles, spruce affectation,   408

Figures pedantical; these summer flies

    Have blown me full of maggot ostentation:

I do forswear them; and I here protest,

    By this white glove,—how white the hand, God
      knows,—   412

Henceforth my wooing mind shall be express'd

    In russet yeas and honest kersey noes:

And, to begin, wench,—so God help me, la!—

393 sound: *swoon*   401 wish: *invite*
405 friend: *mistress*   406 blind harper; *cf. n.*
408 Three-pil'd: *having three piles, superfine*
414 russet: *homespun, homely*   kersey: *coarse woollen, plain*

My love to thee is sound, sans crack or flaw.   416
  Ros. Sans 'sans,' I pray you.
  Ber.   Yet I have a trick
Of the old rage: bear with me, I am sick;
I'll leave it by degrees.   Soft! let us see:
Write, 'Lord have mercy on us' on those three;   420
They are infected, in their hearts it lies;
They have the plague, and caught it of your eyes:
These lords are visited; you are not free,
For the Lord's tokens on you do I see.   424
  Prin. No, they are free that gave these tokens to us.
  Ber. Our states are forfeit: seek not to undo us.
  Ros. It is not so.   For how can this be true,
That you stand forfeit, being those that sue?   428
  Ber. Peace! for I will not have to do with you.
  Ros. Nor shall not, if I do as I intend.
  Ber. Speak for yourselves: my wit is at an end.
  King. Teach us, sweet madam, for our rude trans-
     gression   432
Some fair excuse.
  Prin.   The fairest is confession.
Were you not here, but even now, disguis'd?
  King. Madam, I was.
  Prin.   And were you well advis'd?
  King. I was, fair madam.
  Prin.   When you then were here, 436
What did you whisper in your lady's ear?
  King. That more than all the world I did respect
     her.
  Prin. When she shall challenge this, you will reject
     her.

420 'Lord have mercy'; *cf. n.*   423 visited: *plague-smitten*
424 Lord's tokens: *cf. n.*   426 states: *estates*
428 sue: *equivocally for prosecute and entreat*
435 well advis'd: *in right mind*

King. Upon mine honour, no.

Prin.   Peace! peace! forbear; 440
Your oath once broke, you force not to forswear.

King. Despise me, when I break this oath of mine.

Prin. I will; and therefore keep it. Rosaline,
What did the Russian whisper in your ear?   444

Ros. Madam, he swore that he did hold me dear
As precious eyesight, and did value me
Above this world; adding thereto, moreover,
That he would wed me, or else die my lover.   448

Prin. God give thee joy of him! the noble lord
Most honourably doth uphold his word.

King. What mean you, madam? by my life, my
    troth,
I never swore this lady such an oath.   452

Ros. By heaven you did; and to confirm it plain,
You gave me this: but take it, sir, again.

King. My faith and this the princess I did give:
I knew her by this jewel on her sleeve.   456

Prin. Pardon me, sir, this jewel did she wear;
And Lord Berowne, I thank him, is my dear.
What, will you have me, or your pearl again?

Ber. Neither of either; I remit both twain.   460
I see the trick on 't: here was a consent,
Knowing aforehand of our merriment,
To dash it like a Christmas comedy.
Some   carry-tale,   some   please-man,   some   slight
    zany,   464
Some mumble-news, some trencher-knight, some Dick,
That smiles his cheek in years, and knows the trick
To make my lady laugh when she's dispos'd,

441 force not: *i.e. find it easy*   461 consent: *conspiracy*
463 Christmas comedy: *absurd burlesque*
464 please-man: *flatterer*   zany: *clown*
465 trencher-knight: *serving-man, parasite*
466 years: *i.e. wrinkles, such as belong to years*

Told our intents before; which once disclos'd,   468
The ladies did change favours, and then we,
Following the signs, woo'd but the sign of she.
Now, to our perjury to add more terror,
We are again forsworn, in will and error.   472
Much upon this it is: [*To Boyet.*] and might not you
Forestall our sport, to make us thus untrue?
Do not you know my lady's foot by the squire,
   And laugh upon the apple of her eye?   476
And stand between her back, sir, and the fire,
   Holding a trencher, jesting merrily?
You put our page out: go, you are allow'd;
Die when you will, a smock shall be your shroud.   480
You leer upon me, do you? there's an eye
Wounds like a leaden sword.
   Boyet.   Full merrily
Hath this brave manage, this career, been run.
   Ber. Lo! he is tilting straight.   Peace! I have
   done.   484

      Enter Clown [i.e. Costard].

Welcome, pure wit! thou partest a fair fray.
   Cost. O Lord, sir, they would know
Whether the three Worthies shall come in or no.
   Ber. What, are there but three?
   Cost.   No, sir; but it is vara fine, 488
For every one pursents three.
   Ber.   And three times thrice is nine.
   Cost. Not so, sir; under correction, sir, I hope, it is
   not so.
You cannot beg us, sir, I can assure you, sir; we know
   what we know:

473 upon this: *in this fashion*   475 squire: *square, rule*
476 apple: *pupil*   479 allow'd: *privileged to jest*
483 manage: *horsemanship*   career: *swift encounter of knights*
491 beg us: *prove us fools; cf. n.*

I hope, sir, three times thrice, sir,—

   Ber.   Is not nine? 492

   Cost. Under correction, sir, we know whereuntil it doth amount.

   Ber. By Jove, I always took three threes for nine.

   Cost. O Lord, sir! it were pity you should get 496
your living by reckoning, sir.

   Ber. How much is it?

   Cost. O Lord, sir! the parties themselves, the
actors, sir, will show whereuntil it doth amount: 500
for mine own part, I am, as they say, but to par-
fect one man in one poor man, Pompion the
Great, sir.

   Ber. Art thou one of the Worthies?   504

   Cost. It pleased them to think me worthy of
Pompey the Great: for mine own part, I know
not the degree of the Worthy, but I am to stand
for him.   508

Ber. Go, bid them prepare.

Cost. We will turn it finely off, sir; we will take
   some care.   *Exit.*

King. Berowne, they will shame us; let them not
   approach.

Ber. We are shame-proof, my lord; and 'tis some
   policy   512

To have one show worse than the king's and his company.

King. I say they shall not come.

Prin. Nay, my good lord, let me o'errule you now.

That sport best pleases that doth least know how; 516

Where zeal strives to content, and the contents

Dies in the zeal of that which it presents;

Their form confounded makes most form in mirth,

When great things labouring perish in their birth. 520
Ber. A right description of our sport, my lord.

Enter Braggart [i.e. Armado].

  Arm. Anointed, I implore so much expense
of thy royal sweet breath as will utter a brace of
words.   524

        [Armado converses with the King, and
                  delivers a paper to him.]

  Prin. Doth this man serve God?
  Ber. Why ask you?
  Prin. A' speaks not like a man of God his making.
  Arm. That is all one, my fair, sweet, honey 528
monarch; for, I protest, the schoolmaster is
exceeding fantastical; too-too vain; too-too
vain: but we will put it, as they say, to *fortuna
de la guerra.* I wish you the peace of mind, 532
most royal couplement!   *Exit.*

  King. Here is like to be a good presence of
Worthies. He presents Hector of Troy; the
swain, Pompey the Great; the parish curate, 536
Alexander; Armado's page, Hercules; the pedant, Judas Maccabæus:

And if these four Worthies in their first show thrive,

These four will change habits and present the other
    five.   540

  Ber. There is five in the first show.
  King. You are deceived, 'tis not so.
  Ber. The pedant, the braggart, the hedge-
priest, the fool, and the boy:—   544

Abate throw at novum, and the whole world again

521 our sport: *i.e. the disguise as Muscovites*   527 God his: *God's*
531 fortuna . . . guerra: *the fortune of war*
533 couplement: *couple, pair*
543 hedge-priest: *poor, illiterate priest*
545 Abate . . . novum: *except for a rare throw of the dice; cf. n.*

Cannot pick out five such, take each one in his vein.

  King. The ship is under sail, and here she comes
    amain.

       Enter [Costard armed, for] Pompey.

  Cost. 'I Pompey am,—'
  Boyet.   You lie, you are not he. 548
  Cost. 'I Pompey am,—'
  Boyet.   With libbard's head on knee.
  Ber. Well said, old mocker: I must needs be friends
    with thee.
  Cost. 'I Pompey am, Pompey surnam'd the Big,—'
  Dum. 'The Great.'   552
  Cost. It is 'Great,' sir; 'Pompey surnam'd the Great;
That oft in field, with targe and shield, did make my
    foe to sweat:
And travelling along this coast, I here am come by
    chance,
And lay my arms before the legs of this sweet lass of
    France.'   556
If your ladyship would say, 'Thanks, Pompey,' I had
    done.
  Prin. Great thanks, great Pompey.
  Cost. 'Tis not so much worth; but I hope
I was perfect. I made a little fault in 'Great.' 560
  Ber. My hat to a halfpenny, Pompey proves
the best Worthy.

    Enter Curate [Nathaniel] for Alexander.

Nath. 'When in the world I liv'd, I was the world's
    commander;
  By east, west, north, and south, I spread my con-
    quering might: 564
My scutcheon plain declares that I am Alisander,—'

549 libbard's: *leopard's; cf. n.*

Boyet. Your nose says, no, you are not; for it stands
  too right.

Ber. Your nose smells 'no,' in this, most tender-
  smelling knight.

Prin. The conqueror is dismay'd. Proceed, good
  Alexander.   568

Nath. 'When in the world I liv'd, I was the world's
  commander;—'

Boyet. Most true; 'tis right: you were so, Alisander.

Ber. Pompey the Great,—

Cost. Your servant, and Costard.   572

Ber. Take away the conqueror, take away Alisander.

  Cost. [*To Nathaniel.*] O! sir, you have over-
thrown Alisander the conqueror! You will be
scraped out of the painted cloth for this: your 576
lion, that holds his poll-axe sitting on a close-
stool, will be given to Ajax: he will be the ninth
Worthy. A conqueror, and afeard to speak!
run away for shame, Alisander! [*Nathaniel* 580
retires.] There, an 't shall please you: a foolish
mild man; an honest man, look you, and soon
dashed! He is a marvellous good neighbour,
faith, and a very good bowler; but, for Alisan- 584
der,—alas, you see how 'tis,—a little o'erparted.
But there are Worthies a-coming will speak
their mind in some other sort.

Prin. Stand aside, good Pompey.   588

  Enter Pedant [*Holofernes*] *for Judas, and the
      Boy* [*Moth*] *for Hercules.*

Hol. 'Great Hercules is presented by this imp,
  Whose club kill'd Cerberus, that three-headed *canus;*

---

566 right: *straight; cf. n.*   576 painted cloth; *cf. n.*
577 lion . . . poll-axe; *cf. n.*
585 o'erparted: *i.e. given a part too difficult for him*
590 canus: *canis, dog*

And, when he was a babe, a child, a shrimp,
    Thus did he strangle serpents in his *manus*.   592
Quoniam he seemeth in minority,
Ergo I come with this apology.'
Keep some state in thy exit, and vanish.—

                                  Exit Boy.

'Judas I am.—'   596
   Dum. A Judas!
   Hol. Not Iscariot, sir.
'Judas I am, ycleped Maccabæus.'
   Dum. Judas Maccabæus clipt is plain Judas.   600
   Ber. A kissing traitor. How art thou prov'd Judas?
   Hol. 'Judas I am.—'
   Dum. The more shame for you, Judas.
   Hol. What mean you, sir?   604
   Boyet. To make Judas hang himself.
   Hol. Begin, sir; you are my elder.
   Ber. Well follow'd: Judas was hanged on an elder.
   Hol. I will not be put out of countenance.   608
   Ber. Because thou hast no face.
   Hol. What is this?
   Boyet. A cittern-head.
   Dum. The head of a bodkin.   612
   Ber. A death's face in a ring.
   Long. The face of an old Roman coin, scarce seen.
   Boyet. The pommel of Cæsar's falchion.
   Dum. The carved-bone face on a flask.   616
   Ber. Saint George's half-cheek in a brooch.
   Dum. Ay, and in a brooch of lead.
   Ber. Ay, and worn in the cap of a toothdrawer.

592 manus: *hands*
594 Ergo: *therefore*
607 elder; *cf. n.*
612 bodkin: *small dagger*
616 flask: *powder flask*

593 Quoniam: *since*
601 A kissing traitor; *cf. n.*
611 cittern: *cithern, guitar*
613 death's face: *death's head*
619 toothdrawer; *cf. n.*

And now forward; for we have put thee in coun-
  tenance.   620
  Hol. You have put me out of countenance.
  Ber. False: we have given thee faces.
  Hol. But you have outfaced them all.
  Ber. An thou wert a lion, we would do so.   624
  Boyet. Therefore, as he is an ass, let him go.
And so adieu, sweet Jude! nay, why dost thou stay?
  Dum. For the later end of his name.
  Ber. For the ass to the Jude? give it him:—Jud-as,
  away!   628
  Hol. This is not generous, not gentle, not humble.
  Boyet. A light for Monsieur Judas! it grows dark,
  he may stumble.   [*Hol. retires.*]
  Prin. Alas! poor Maccabæus, how hath he been
  baited.

  Enter Braggart [*i.e. Armado, for Hector*].

  Ber. Hide thy head, Achilles: here comes 632
Hector in arms.
  Dum. Though my mocks come home by me,
I will now be merry.
  King. Hector was but a Troyan in respect of 636
this.
  Boyet. But is this Hector?
  King. I think Hector was not so clean-tim-
bered.   640
  Long. His calf is too big for Hector's.
  Dum. More calf, certain.
  Boyet. No; he is best indued in the small.
  Ber. This cannot be Hector.   **644**
  Dum. He's a god or a painter; for he makes
faces.

634 by: *about, near*   636 Troyan: *Trojan, contemptible fellow*
640 clean-timbered: *well-built*   643 small: *small of the leg*

Arm. 'The armipotent Mars, of lances the almighty,
Gave Hector a gift,—'   648

    Dum. A gilt nutmeg.

    Ber. A lemon.

    Long. Stuck with cloves.

    Dum. No, cloven.   652

    Arm. Peace!

'The armipotent Mars, of lances the almighty,
   Gave Hector a gift, the heir of Ilion;
A man so breath'd, that certain he would fight ye   656
   From morn till night, out of his pavilion.
I am that flower,—'

    Dum.   That mint.

    Long.   That columbine.

    Arm. Sweet Lord Longaville, rein thy tongue.

    Long. I must rather give it the rein, for it 660
runs against Hector.

    Dum. Ay, and Hector's a greyhound.

    Arm. The sweet war-man is dead and rotten;
sweet chucks, beat not the bones of the buried; 664
when he breathed, he was a man. But I will forward with my device. [*To the Princess.*] Sweet
royalty, bestow on me the sense of hearing.

                                Berowne steps forth.

    Prin. Speak, brave Hector; we are much de- 668
lighted.

    Arm. I do adore thy sweet Grace's slipper.

    Boyet. [*Aside to Dumaine.*] Loves her by the
foot.   672

    Dum. [*Aside to Boyet.*] He may not by the
yard.

    Arm. 'This Hector far surmounted Hannibal,—'

        [*Berowne returns with Costard.*]

656 breath'd: *endowed with breath, vigorous*

Cost. The party is gone; fellow Hector, she is 676
gone; she is two months on her way.

Arm. What meanest thou?

Cost. Faith, unless you play the honest Troyan, the poor wench is cast away: she's quick; 680
the child brags in her belly already: 'tis yours.

Arm. Dost thou infamonize me among po-
tentates? Thou shalt die.

Cost. Then shall Hector be whipped for Ja- 684
quenetta that is quick by him, and hanged for
Pompey that is dead by him.

Dum. Most rare Pompey!

Boyet. Renowned Pompey!   688

Ber. Greater than great, great, great, great
Pompey! Pompey the Huge!

Dum. Hector trembles.

Ber. Pompey is moved. More Ates, more 692
Ates! stir them on! stir them on!

Dum. Hector will challenge him.

Ber. Ay, if a' have no more man's blood in 's
belly than will sup a flea.   696

Arm. By the north pole, I do challenge thee.

Cost. I will not fight with a pole, like a
northern man: I'll slash; I'll do it by the
sword. I bepray you, let me borrow my arms 700
again.

Dum. Room for the incensed Worthies!

Cost. I'll do it in my shirt.

Dum. Most resolute Pompey!   704

Moth. Master, let me take you a button-hole
lower. Do you not see, Pompey is uncasing for

676 party: *i.e. Jaquenetta*   682 infamonize: *infamize*
692 Ates: *mischief; cf. n.*
699 northern man: *countryman from the north, boor*
705 take . . . lower: (1) *help you to strip,* (2) *humiliate you*

the combat? What mean you? you will lose
your reputation.   708

Arm. Gentlemen and soldiers, pardon me; I
will not combat in my shirt.

Dum. You may not deny it; Pompey hath
made the challenge.   712

Arm. Sweet bloods, I both may and will.

Ber. What reason have you for 't?

Arm. The naked truth of it is, I have no
shirt. I go woolward for penance.   716

Boyet. True, and it was enjoined him in Rome
for want of linen; since when, I'll be sworn, he
wore none but a dish-clout of Jaquenetta's, and
that a' wears next his heart for a favour.   720

Enter a Messenger, Monsieur Marcade.

Mar. God save you, madam!

Prin. Welcome, Marcade;
But that thou interrupt'st our merriment.

Mar. I am sorry, madam; for the news I bring   724
Is heavy in my tongue. The king your father—

Prin. Dead, for my life!

Mar. Even so: my tale is told.

Ber. Worthies, away! The scene begins to 728
cloud.

Arm. For mine own part, I breathe free breath.
I have seen the day of wrong through the little
hole of discretion, and I will right myself like a 732
soldier.   *Exeunt Worthies.*

King. How fares your majesty?

Prin. Boyet, prepare: I will away to-night.

King. Madam, not so: I do beseech you, stay.   736

Prin. Prepare, I say. I thank you, gracious lords,

716 woolward: *i.e. with wool, instead of linen, next to the skin*
732 hole of discretion; *cf. n.*

For all your fair endeavours; and entreat,
Out of a new-sad soul, that you vouchsafe
In your rich wisdom to excuse or hide   740
The liberal opposition of our spirits,
If over-boldly we have borne ourselves
In the converse of breath; your gentleness
Was guilty of it. Farewell, worthy lord!   744
A heavy heart bears not a humble tongue,
Excuse me so, coming too short of thanks
For my great suit so easily obtain'd.

    King. The extreme parts of time extremely
      forms   748
All causes to the purpose of his speed,
And often, at his very loose, decides
That which long process could not arbitrate:
And though the mourning brow of progeny   752
Forbid the smiling courtesy of love
The holy suit which fain it would convince;
Yet, since love's argument was first on foot,
Let not the cloud of sorrow justle it   756
From what it purpos'd; since, to wail friends lost
Is not by much so wholesome-profitable
As to rejoice at friends but newly found.

    Prin. I understand you not: my griefs are
      double.   760

    Ber. Honest plain words best pierce the ear of
      grief;
And by these badges understand the king.
For your fair sakes have we neglected time,
Play'd foul play with our oaths. Your beauty,
    ladies,   764

741 liberal: *over-free*   743 converse of breath: *conversation*
745 humble: *suited to the offering of thanks and apologies*
748, 749 *Cf. n.*   750 loose: *loosing, parting*
754 convince: *give proof of*   760 double: *excessive* (?)
762 badges; *cf. n.*

Hath much deform'd us, fashioning our humours
Even to the opposed end of our intents;
And what in us hath seem'd ridiculous,—
As love is full of unbefitting strains;   768
All wanton as a child, skipping and vain;
Form'd by the eye, and, therefore, like the eye,
Full of straying shapes, of habits and of forms,
Varying in subjects, as the eye doth roll   772
To every varied object in his glance:—
Which parti-coated presence of loose love
Put on by us, if, in your heavenly eyes,
Have misbecom'd our oaths and gravities,   776
Those heavenly eyes, that look into these faults,
Suggested us to make. Therefore, ladies,
Our love being yours, the error that love makes
Is likewise yours: we to ourselves prove false,   780
By being once false for ever to be true
To those that make us both,—fair ladies, you:
And even that falsehood, in itself a sin,
Thus purifies itself and turns to grace.   784

   Prin. We have receiv'd your letters full of love;
Your favours, the embassadors of love;
And, in our maiden council, rated them
At courtship, pleasant jest, and courtesy,   788
As bombast and as lining to the time.
But more devout than this in our respects
Have we not been; and therefore met your loves
In their own fashion, like a merriment.   792

    Dum. Our letters, madam, show'd much more than
     jest.

    Long. So did our looks.

766 *In a way quite opposite to our intentions*
768 strains: *impulses*   774 parti-coated: *motley-coated*
778 Suggested: *tempted*   789 bombast: *padding*
790 devout: *serious*   respects: *reflections*

   Ros.   We did not quote them so.

   King. Now, at the latest minute of the hour,
Grant us your loves.

   Prin.   A time, methinks, too short 796
To make a world-without-end bargain in.
No, no, my lord, your Grace is perjur'd much,
Full of dear guiltiness; and therefore this:
If for my love,—as there is no such cause,—   800
You will do aught, this shall you do for me:
Your oath I will not trust; but go with speed
To some forlorn and naked hermitage,
Remote from all the pleasures of the world;   804
There stay, until the twelve celestial signs
Have brought about the annual reckoning.
If this austere insociable life
Change not your offer made in heat of blood;   808
If frosts and fasts, hard lodging and thin weeds,
Nip not the gaudy blossoms of your love,
But that it bear this trial and last love;
Then, at the expiration of the year,   812
Come challenge me, challenge me by these deserts,
And, by this virgin palm now kissing thine,
I will be thine; and, till that instant, shut
My woful self up in a mourning house,   816
Raining the tears of lamentation
For the remembrance of my father's death.
If this thou do deny, let our hands part;
Neither intitled in the other's heart.   820
King. If this, or more than this, I would deny,
   To flatter up these powers of mine with rest,
The sudden hand of death close up mine eye!

794 quote: *cf. IV. iii. 87*   799 dear: *amiable*
806 *Completed the twelve months of the year*
809 weeds: *clothing*   811 last: *remain*
820 intitled: *having any right*

Hence ever then my heart is in thy breast. 824
Ber. And what to me, my love? and what to me?
Ros. You must be purged too, your sins are rack'd:
You are attaint with faults and perjury;
Therefore, if you my favour mean to get, 828
A twelvemonth shall you spend, and never rest,
But seek the weary beds of people sick.
Dum. But what to me, my love? but what to me?
Kath. A wife! A beard, fair health, and
honesty; 832
With three-fold love I wish you all these three.
Dum. O! shall I say, I thank you, gentle wife?
Kath. Not so, my lord. A twelvemonth and a day
I'll mark no words that smooth-fac'd wooers say: 836
Come when the king doth to my lady come;
Then, if I have much love, I'll give you some.
Dum. I'll serve thee true and faithfully till then.
Kath. Yet swear not, lest ye be forsworn again. 840
Long. What says Maria?
Mar. At the twelvemonth's end
I'll change my black gown for a faithful friend.
Long. I'll stay with patience; but the time is long.
Mar. The liker you; few taller are so young. 844
Ber. Studies my lady? mistress, look on me.
Behold the window of my heart, mine eye,
What humble suit attends thy answer there;
Impose some service on me for thy love. 848
Ros. Oft have I heard of you, my Lord Berowne,
Before I saw you; and the world's large tongue
Proclaims you for a man replete with mocks,
Full of comparisons and wounding flouts, 852

824 *Cf. n.*
826 rack'd: *i.e. unnaturally extended*
844 liker; *cf. n.*
852 comparisons: *personalities*

825-830 *Cf. n.*
843 stay: *wait*
850 large: *lavish*

Which you on all estates will execute
That lie within the mercy of your wit:
To weed this wormwood from your fruitful brain,
And therewithal to win me, if you please,—   856
Without the which I am not to be won,—
You shall this twelvemonth term, from day to day,
Visit the speechless sick, and still converse
With groaning wretches; and your task shall be   860
With all the fierce endeavour of your wit
To enforce the pained impotent to smile.

   Ber. To move wild laughter in the throat of death?
It cannot be; it is impossible: 864
Mirth cannot move a soul in agony.

   Ros. Why, that's the way to choke a gibing spirit,
Whose influence is begot of that loose grace
Which shallow laughing hearers give to fools.   868
A jest's prosperity lies in the ear
Of him that hears it, never in the tongue
Of him that makes it: then, if sickly ears,
Deaf'd with the clamours of their own dear groans, 872
Will hear your idle scorns, continue then,
And I will have you and that fault withal;
But if they will not, throw away that spirit,
And I shall find you empty of that fault,   876
Right joyful of your reformation.

   Ber. A twelvemonth! well, befall what will befall,
I'll jest a twelvemonth in an hospital.

   Prin. [*To the King.*] Ay, sweet my lord; and so I
    take my leave.   880

   King. No, madam; we will bring you on your way.

   Ber. Our wooing doth not end like an old play;
Jack hath not Jill; these ladies' courtesy

---

853 estates: *ranks*   865 agony: *i.e. of death*
872 dear: *intense*   874 withal: *also*   881 bring: *attend*

Might well have made our sport a comedy.   884

  King. Come, sir, it wants a twelvemonth and a day,
And then 'twill end.

  Ber.   That's too long for a play.

          Enter Braggart [Armado].

  Arm. Sweet majesty, vouchsafe me,—

  Prin. Was not that Hector?   888

  Dum. The worthy knight of Troy.

  Arm. I will kiss thy royal finger, and take
leave. I am a votary; I have vowed to Jaquenetta to hold the plough for her sweet love three 892
year. But, most esteemed greatness, will you
hear the dialogue that the two learned men have
compiled in praise of the owl and the cuckoo? it
should have followed in the end of our show.   896

  King. Call them forth quickly; we will do so.

  Arm. Holla! approach.

              Enter all.

This side is *Hiems,* Winter; this *Ver,* the Spring;
the one maintained by the owl, th' other by the 900
cuckoo. *Ver,* begin.

             The Song.

             [Spring.]

'When daisies pied and violets blue
    And lady-smocks all silver-white
And cuckoo-buds of yellow hue   904
    Do paint the meadows with delight,
The cuckoo then, on every tree,
Mocks married men; for thus sings he,
                     Cuckoo;   908

899 *Cf. n.*   903 lady-smocks: *cardamine pratensis, May-flower*
904 cuckoo-buds: *buttercups or cowslips*

Cuckoo, cuckoo: O, word of fear,
Unpleasing to a married ear!

'When shepherds pipe on oaten straws,
    And merry larks are ploughmen's clocks,   912
When turtles tread, and rooks, and daws,
    And maidens bleach their summer smocks,
The cuckoo then, on every tree,
Mocks married men; for thus sings he,   916
                Cuckoo;
Cuckoo, cuckoo: O, word of fear,
Unpleasing to a married ear!'

Winter.

'When icicles hang by the wall,   920
    And Dick the shepherd blows his nail,
And Tom bears logs into the hall,
    And milk comes frozen home in pail,
When blood is nipp'd, and ways be foul,   924
Then nightly sings the staring owl,
                Tu-who;
Tu-whit, tu-who—a merry note,
While greasy Joan doth keel the pot.   928

'When all aloud the wind doth blow,
    And coughing drowns the parson's saw,
And birds sit brooding in the snow,
    And Marian's nose looks red and raw,   932
When roasted crabs hiss in the bowl,
Then nightly sings the staring owl,
                Tu-who;
Tu-whit, tu-who—a merry note,   936
While greasy Joan doth keel the pot.'

913 turtles: *turtle-doves*   928 keel: *cool by stirring*
930 saw: *maxim or wise talk*
933 crabs: *wild, sour apples*   bowl: *i.e. wassail-bowl*

Arm. The words of Mercury are harsh after the songs of Apollo. You, that way: we, this way. 940

Exeunt Omnes.

FINIS.

NOTES

Dramatis Personæ. A list of characters for this play was first supplied by Rowe in 1709. Berowne (spelled 'Biron' in the second and later Folios and in most modern editions) is accented on the second syllable, and rimes with 'moon' (cf. IV. iii. 232). Longaville rimes with 'ill' (IV. iii. 123) but sometimes also with 'compile' (IV. iii. 133) and with 'mile' (V. ii. 53). Boyet rimes with 'debt' (V. ii. 335); Rosaline with 'mine' (IV. i. 53) and 'thine' (V. ii. 133). Moth was probably pronounced as if spelled 'Mote' (cf. IV. iii. 161, where the common noun, mote, is spelled 'Moth' in the early editions). Armado is often spelled 'Armatho,' which probably indicates the pronunciation (Spanish d = th).

Unusual irregularities are found in the quarto and folio editions of *Love's Labour's Lost* in the naming of the characters. The confusion is particularly striking in IV. ii, where the names of Holofernes and Nathaniel are transposed through most of the scene. Throughout the play the Princess is often called 'Queen'; and the names of Armado, Holofernes, Nathaniel, Costard, and Dull are erratically supplanted in stage directions and speech headings by the titles, Braggart, Pedant, Curate, Clown, and Constable, while Moth is often referred to as Page or Boy. Some recent editors have attempted to discriminate on the evidence of these phenomena between the original and the revised portions of the play. Thus Mr. Dover Wilson argues that passages using the designations 'Braggart,' 'Pedant,' etc., belong to the revision of 1597, whereas passages that give the proper names 'Armado,' 'Holofernes,' etc., are part of the original play. But this leads to risky conclusions.

Love's Labour's Lost. The spelling of the title is that of the third Folio. The earlier Folios have Loues Labour's Lost. The first Quarto has on the title-page Loues labors lost, but as running-title *Loues Labor's lost.* 'Labour's' was evidently intended as a contraction of 'Labour is.' Meres, however, referred to the play as *Loue labors lost,* clearly regarding 'labors' as the nominative plural. Likewise the play is known in France as *Les Peines de l'Amour Perdues* and in Germany as *Verlorene Liebesmüh.*

I. i. 12. *Navarre shall be the wonder of the world.* The opening speech of the King shows the influence of Marlowe's versification in its special sonorousness, alliteration, and exhilaration. Compare with the present line Marlowe's *Dido,* l. 730: 'Lest I be made a wonder to the world.'

I. i. 14. *Still and contemplative in living art.* Quietly contemplating the art of perfect living. The line alludes to the common mediæval distinction between the contemplative and the active life. Mr. J. S. Reid (Iowa *Philological Quarterly,* July, 1922) suggests that 'living art' refers particularly to the Stoic term, *ars vivendi,* ethical (as distinguished from physical and logical) philosophy.

I. i. 62. *feast.* Theobald's emendation for the 'fast' of the early editions.

I. i. 67, 68. *If study's gain be thus, and this be so, Study knows that which yet it doth not know.* If the benefit of study consist only in the development of casuistry, then there is no such thing as knowledge: instead of discovering the true, study merely merges the true and the false.

I. i. 73. *Which, with pain purchas'd, doth inherit pain.* In which the final result of painful striving is only further pain.

I. i. 80-83. *Study me how to please the eye indeed, By fixing it upon a fairer eye, Who dazzling so, that eye shall be his heed, And give him light that it was blinded by.* 'Me' (l. 80) is the 'ethical dative'; 'Who' (l. 82) refers to the eye mentioned in l. 80 or to its owner; and 'it' (l. 83) is the object of 'by.' The passage may be paraphrased: Rather study how really to please your eye by fixing it upon that of a sweetheart, whereupon your own eye will be dimmed; but the 'fairer eye' will be your sole attention and give light to you whom it has blinded.

I. i. 88-93. *These earthly godfathers of heaven's lights, That give a name to every fixed star, Have no more profit of their shining nights Than those that walk and wot not what they are. Too much to know is to know nought but fame; And every godfather can give a name.* The learned astronomers who give names to the stars have no more real control of them than have the ignorant. Encyclopedic knowledge is but parrot-like, no more essential than the bestowal of a name at the baptism of an infant.

I. i. 95. *Proceeded.* Almost certainly used in the technical sense of taking an academic degree. Berowne employs his own intellectual subtlety to discourage others from similarly training themselves.

I. i. 99. *In reason nothing. Ber. Something, then, in rime.* Shakespeare is very fond of playing on the alliterative phrase, rime and reason. Compare I. ii. 113.

I. i. 106. *May's new-fangled shows.* Since the rest of the passage is in alternate rime, it is assumed that the poet intended this line to end with a word riming with 'birth' (l. 104). Many editors have therefore substituted 'earth' (Theobald) or 'mirth' (Walker) for 'shows'; but neither seems natural, and it is quite likely that Shakespeare himself made the slip through inadvertence.

I. i. 109. *Climb o'er the house to unlock the little gate.* Take an absurdly impractical course. The line is printed as in the Quarto. The Folio has the inferior version: 'That were to clymbe ore the house to vnlocke the gate.'

I. i. 114. *Yet confident I'll keep what I have sworn.* The second Folio reads 'swore,' which most modern editors introduce for the sake of rime.

I. ii. 58. *the dancing horse.* A famous performing horse named Morocco, first definitely mentioned in 1591 but apparently known as early as 1589. He was particularly accomplished in arithmetic.

I. ii. 83. *Of what complexion?* The four 'complexions' of the body were variously ascribed to the four elements (earth, air, water, fire) and to the four 'humours' (phlegm, choler, blood, melancholy).

I. ii. 95. *she had a green wit.* Perhaps Moth implies a pun on the green withes with which Samson was bound (Judges 16. 7): 'And Samson said unto her, If they bind me with seven green withs that were never dried, then shall I be weak, and be as another man.'

I. ii. 115, 116. *a ballet . . . of the King and the Beggar.* The ballad of King Cophetua and the Beggar-maid is a favorite subject of allusion in Shakespeare and his contemporaries. Compare Armado's later mention of it in his letter (IV. i. 65 ff.). The extant version, printed in Percy's *Reliques,* appears to be post-Elizabethan.

I. ii. 167. *the merry days of desolation.* Perhaps Costard means 'dissipation.'

II. i. 41. *Lord Perigort.* Of course, an invented name. Périgord, near Bordeaux, was an important district during the Hundred Years' War between France and England. Shakespeare would have found it mentioned repeatedly in Holinshed in connection with the French campaigns of Henry VI's reign. Falconbridge, in the next line, appears to have been a name the poet liked. It is not French, but is applied to important characters both in *King John* and in *3 Henry VI*. See note on the latter play, I. i. 239, in this edition.

II. i. 62, 63. *And much too little of that good I saw Is my report to his great worthiness.* My testimony to his worthiness is summed up in saying that I had much too little opportunity to observe it.

II. i. 74. *That aged ears play truant at his tales.* The aged are tempted away from business to listen to his tales.

II. i. 130. *Being but the one half of an entire sum.* That is, the sum which Navarre's father had lent to France amounted to two hundred thousand crowns. See Appendix A, p. 130.

II. i. 184. *let it blood.* Alluding to the nearly inevitable practice of blood-letting in sickness.

II. i. 188. *No point.* A pun on the English word, 'point' (i.e. my eye is not sharp enough), and the French negative, *ne . . . point.* Maria makes the same poor joke in V. ii. 278.

II. i. 193. *The heir of Alençon, Katharine her name.* Both the Quarto and Folio texts here print 'Rosalin' instead of Katharine, and in line 208 'Katherin(e)' instead of Rosaline. This is one of the chief points used by Mr. Dover Wilson in an ingenious elaboration of a theory proposed by Mr. Charlton in 1917 (*The Library,* vol. viii, pp. 355-370); namely, that Shakespeare, in the first version of the play, intended the ladies to be masked and Boyet to mix their names when the lovers inquire of him, and that in the revised version he intended to omit this motive of confused identity because of its employment later in V. ii. Mr. Wilson thinks that an unintentional blending of the two versions can be seen in the text of the present scene. There are very strong reasons against these assumptions. The only basis for the idea that the three ladies (unlike the

Princess) wear masks in this scene is Berowne's ex-
clamation, 'Now fair befall your mask!' (l. 123), and
the reply of Rosaline ('Katharine' in the Quarto).
This is far from conclusive. On the other hand, the
evident purpose of the scene is to allow each of the
lords an opportunity of falling in love with a lady
with whom, by hypothesis, he has previously had only
the slightest acquaintance, but with whose peculiari-
ties of face and coloring they are all shown to be per-
fectly familiar when they next appear (see Berowne's
soliloquy, III. i. 205 ff., and the whole of IV. iii). It
is impossible to believe that any author, skilled or un-
skilled, could have had the idea of frustrating so
essential a piece of dramatic business by having the
ladies unrecognizably masked and making them converse at cross purposes with the wrong gallants.

II. i. 201. *God's blessing on your beard.* Longaville means to imply that Boyet's flippant answers are
inconsistent with his venerable beard. In pronunciation 'beard' and 'heard' rimed better than at present,
the latter word still retaining the long vowel of its
infinitive.

II. i. 212. *Farewell to me, sir, and welcome to you.*
Say 'farewell' to me, and I will say you are welcome
(to depart).

II. i. 217. *Kath. Two hot sheeps, marry.* The
Quarto assigns this speech to 'Lady Ka.' and the
Folio to 'La. Ma.' Nearly all editors follow the latter,
which, however, is probably a compositor's error
occasioned by the fact that Maria is the speaker just
above (l. 213). The three following lady's speeches
(ll. 219, 220, 222), assigned in both the early editions
simply to 'La.' or 'Lad.,' evidently belong to the same
lady who speaks in l. 217. The Quarto's introduction
of Katharine into the conversation is a dramatic gain.

II. i. 221. *My lips are no common, though several
they be.* A quasi-legal pun. Several land, as op-

posed to common, was that in separate or private ownership. Katharine also calls her lips several as being more than one, or as being parted.

II. i. 244. *margent.* Alluding to the habit of printing explanatory notes on the margin (rather than the foot) of the page.

III. i. 3. *Concolinel.* Not satisfactorily explained. It has been interpreted as a corruption of the Irish words 'Can cailin gheal' (pronounced con colleen yal), i.e. 'sing, maiden fair.' Marshall suggests that it is French, 'Quand Colinelle,' which is at least as likely.

III. i. 9. *brawl.* French *branle.* Defined as the oldest of figure dances.

III. i. 13. *canary.* The canary was a very lively dance, allowing the improvisation of new steps.

III. i. 32. *The hobby-horse is forgot.* The 'hobby-horse,' a dancer made up to look like a horse, was a favorite figure in morris dances, and a special subject of Puritan invective. The line, 'O, the hobby-horse is forgot,' which Shakespeare uses again in *Hamlet,* III. ii. 145, has been supposed to come from a ballad.

III. i. 75. *no salve in the mail, sir.* That is, no quacksalver's remedy. Costard apprehends that Armado is calling for exotic (and hence suspect) remedies for the broken shin.

III. i. 86. *is not l'envoy a salve?* A pun on the Latin *salve,* used in salutations. The *envoi,* or concluding section, of a mediæval *ballade* ordinarily contained an address to the person to whom the poem was written.

III. i. 107. *The boy hath sold him a bargain.* This is usually explained as 'has got the better of him, made a fool of him,'—a sense which the idiom, to sell one a bargain, undoubtedly had. But I think the context shows that Costard, in the innocence of his rustic heart, really conjectures that *l'envoy* means goose, and that the goose mentioned in the incomprehensible

speeches he has just listened to is a veritable bird,
over the price of which Armado and Moth have been
haggling.

III. i. 116. *And he ended the market.* There was
a proverb: 'Three women and a goose make a market.'

III. i. 185. *A very beadle to a humorous sigh.* The
beadle was an inferior kind of constable who whipped
small offenders. See *2 Henry VI* II. i. 135. 'Humorous' is here used in the sense of sentimental.

III. i. 190. *This senior-junior, giant-dwarf, Dan
Cupid.* The early editions, both quarto and folio, read
'This signior Iunios giant-dwarf, dan Cupid.' It may
be better, instead of Hanmer's emendation as given in
the text, to print with Hart: 'This signior junior,' i.e.
Mr. Youngster.

IV. i. 22. *O heresy in fair, fit for these days!*
The recent Cambridge editors, following a suggestion
of Hart, see in this line and in lines 30-33 below 'a
direct allusion to the conversion of Henry IV' to
Romanism, July, 1593. The detached lines mentioned fit the historical situation well enough, but the
Princess' speech as a whole does not. In his early
plays Shakespeare is very fond of introducing passages of reflective moralizing such as this, generally
without any suggestion of topical interest.

IV. i. 48. *The thickest, and the tallest.* As Marshall remarks, Costard's otherwise dull and uncivil
joke gains point if one remembers that the ladies'
parts were performed by boys. The wit apparently
lies in the fact that the Princess was represented by
the oldest and stoutest of this group, whose figure
was outgrowing its suitability to feminine rôles.

IV. i. 56. *Break up this capon.* To break up a
fowl was to carve it. Capon is used figuratively, like
the French *poulet,* for a love-letter.

IV. i. 91. *the Nemean lion.* The lion slain by
Hercules in performance of his first labor. Here and

in *Hamlet* I. iv. 83 Shakespeare erroneously accents the first syllable. Hart notes that Golding's Ovid gave him a precedent for the pronunciation.

IV. i. 102. *Monarcho.* 'The monarch'; a crazy Italian who lived about the English court. He was subject to delusions of grandeur, and though he died about 1580, was still a familiar subject of allusion twenty years later.

IV. i. 112. *she that bears the bow.* Rosaline is punning on 'shooter' and 'suitor,' which were pronounced alike, and often quibblingly confused. In Boyet's speech, line 111, the early editions all print 'shooter' for 'suitor.' In Shakespeare's time, it should be remembered, firearms had not replaced the bow in the fashionable sport of deer-slaying. Several writers see a special application in the deer-shooting allusions of this and the next scene to Queen Elizabeth's well-known fondness for the cross-bow. Cf. Appendix A, p. 128, note 1.

IV. i. 115. *if horns that year miscarry.* If the crop of horns is not good. Boyet succumbs to the inevitable jest about cuckolds' horns, produced by unfaithful wives.

IV. i. 123. *King Pepin of France.* Charlemagne's father, a very ancient monarch.

IV. ii. 32. *So were there a patch set on learning, to see him in a school.* The word 'patch' is used ambiguously. If Dull were seen in a school, (1) a patch (fool) would be put to study, and (2) a patch (disfigurement, disgrace) would be put on learning.

IV. ii. 34. *Many can brook the weather that love not the wind.* Apparently a proverbial saying, similar to 'There is no accounting for tastes,' or 'It takes many sorts of men to make a world.' To brook the weather means to put up with foul weather.

IV. ii. 37. *Dictynna.* This rare epithet of Diana is found in Golding's Ovid and in Tottel's Miscellany.

It made trouble for the early compositors, who spell it 'Dictisima' and 'Dictima.'

IV. ii. 42. *The allusion holds in the exchange.* That is, the point of the jest is still seen when Holofernes recasts (in ll. 40, 41) the form in which Dull has given it (l. 36).

IV. ii. 82. *vir sapit qui pauca loquitur.* That man is wise who speaks little. The sentence is borrowed directly from Lyly's Latin grammar.

IV. ii. 96-98. *Fauste, precor gelida quando pecus omne sub umbra Ruminat . . . good old Mantuan.* Holofernes quotes the opening words of the first eclogue of Mantuanus (Baptista Spagnuoli of Mantua, d. 1516), whose Latin poems were an elementary textbook in the schools of the day. The early editions read 'Facile' instead of 'Fauste,' which the recent Cambridge editors think an intentional misquotation. It is more probably a compositor's misreading of Shakespeare's manuscript.

IV. ii. 100, 101. *Venetia, Venetia, Chi non te vede, non te pretia.* Archaic Italian: 'Venice, Venice, he who has not seen thee cannot value thee.' The words are gibberish as they appear in the early editions. Theobald first explained them.

IV. ii. 103, 104. *Ut, re, sol, la, mi, fa.* Notes of the old musical scale in incorrect order. They should run: 'ut (later replaced by "do"), re, mi, fa, sol, la.'

IV. ii. 105. *As Horace says in his ——.* What saying of Horace Holofernes has in mind the commentators have failed to discover.

IV. ii. 124. *You find not the apostrophas.* You pronounce syllables which should be omitted. Or perhaps, as Gollancz suggests, Holofernes means the reverse (diereses): You omit syllables which should be pronounced.

IV. ii. 126. *numbers ratified.* Metre sanctioned by convention.

IV. ii. 136. *from one Monsieur Berowne, one of the strange queen's lords.* A very confusing and probably corrupt passage. What Jaquenetta here says is directly opposed to her assertion (ll. 94, 95) that the letter was sent to her from Don Armado; and the designation of Berowne as 'one of the strange queen's lords' is equally absurd. The recent Cambridge editors add another to a great list of implausible explanations by theorizing that 'Berowne' is a compositor's error for 'Boyet' (written 'Bo' or 'Boy'), and that Jaquenetta understands Holofernes to mean by 'directed' imparted. They assume, therefore, that Boyet juggled the two letters.

IV. ii. 147. *Trip and go.* A common phrase, borrowed from the words of a popular morris dance song.

IV. ii. 169, 170. *society—saith the text—is the happiness of life.* Nathaniel's source for the remark has not been found. Perhaps he is inventing the 'text' like the 'certain Father' of line 155. There is a much quoted Latin hexameter line, repeated by Marlowe in *Doctor Faustus,* which may have been in Shakespeare's mind: 'Solamen miseris socios habuisse doloris,' it is a comfort to the wretched to have companions in their pain.

IV. iii. 7. *as mad as Ajax: it kills sheep.* Alluding to the story that Ajax, disappointed of the award of Achilles' armor, went mad and attacked a flock of sheep, which he took for a hostile army.

IV. iii. 89. *Stoop, I say.* 'Stoop' is generally explained as equivalent to stooping, crooked; but there seems no justification for such a use. It is probably the verbal imperative, addressed *sotto voce* to Dumaine: Come off your stilts, abandon your exalted nonsense.

IV. iii. 180. *With men like men, men of inconstancy.* There is little to choose between many of the emendations of this line, which is clearly imperfect

both in metre and in sense as printed in the early
editions: 'With men like men of inconstancie.' The
reading here accepted, which appears to be original
with Craig, makes the line mean 'with ordinary, in-
constant men.'

IV. iii. 212. *sirs.* Costard and Jaquenetta are addressed. Shakespeare uses 'sirs' of women alone in
Antony and Cleopatra IV. xiii. 85.

IV. iii. 255. *the school of night.* Perhaps 'that
which teaches night to be what it is: dark and sinister.'
Most editors have preferred to adopt an emendation
that originated with Theobald and Warburton: the
scowl of night. The recent Cambridge editors lend
their support to a fantastic notion of Mr. Acheson to
the effect that 'the school of night' is a topical allusion
to a society composed of Sir Walter Raleigh, the poet
Chapman, Marlowe, etc., whom it is supposed Shakespeare was ridiculing in this play.

IV. iii. 256. *And beauty's crest becomes the
heavens well.* An obscure line. The most obvious
meaning is rather flat: 'And beauty's distinguishing
mark (or perfection) well becomes the regions of
light.'

IV. iii. 257. *Devils soonest tempt, resembling
spirits of light.* Perhaps an allusion to 2 Corinthians
11. 14: 'And no marvel, for Satan himself is transformed into an angel of light.' The idea recurs in
Hamlet II. ii. 636, 637, and in *Measure for Measure*
II. iv. 16, 17.

IV. iii. 299-304. The wording and argument of
these lines are repeated in more extended form later
in the speech. Compare especially lines 320-323 and
350-354. It is generally recognized that an earlier
and a later, expanded and improved, version of the
same speech have been accidentally amalgamated in
the text which reached the printers. Mr. Dover Wilson argues that the opening lines of Berowne (289-

295) were intended to begin both versions, and that they were followed in the earlier version by ll. 296-317 and in the later by ll. 318-365. See note on V. ii. 825-830.

IV. iii. 305. *poisons up.* Completely poisons. Theobald's emendation, 'prisons up,' is plausible and has been adopted by many editors.

IV. iii. 306. *The nimble spirits in the arteries.* The arteries were supposed to contain, not blood simply, but 'vital spirits.'

IV. iii. 336. *When the suspicious head of theft is stopp'd.* The 'suspicious head of theft' may be interpreted either actively, i.e. the acutely watchful ears of a thief; or passively, i.e. the ears of one suspicious of being robbed. I think the former the more likely.

IV. iii. 364. *For charity itself fulfils the law.* Cf. Romans 13. 8: 'for he that loveth another hath fulfilled the law.'

IV. iii. 383. *Sow'd cockle reap'd no corn.* An elliptical and proverbial expression: if we plant weeds, we shall not reap corn; unless we make the proper preparations, we shall not gain the desired results.

V. i. 22. *to speak 'dout,' fine, when he should say, 'doubt.'* Holofernes belongs to the pedantic group which sought during the Renaissance to bring the spelling and pronunciation of English words as close as possible to the real or fancied Latin original. Thus the earlier *doute* was written and sounded *doubt* on the authority of Latin *dubitum,* and the earlier *dette* made into *debt* on the analogy of Latin *debitum.* The new, unhistorical spellings managed to establish themselves, but not the pronunciations upon which Holofernes and his class insisted.

V. i. 31. *Priscian a little scratched.* That is, your Latin is passable, but hackneyed. Priscian wrote, during the fifth century A.D., works which were long

the standard textbooks on Latin grammar. Previous
editors have assumed that 'scratched Priscian' must be
equivalent to 'breaking Priscian's head,' i.e. speaking
ungrammatical Latin. Hence Theobald misingen-
iously invented an error by changing Sir Nathaniel's
correct sentence to 'Laus deo, *bone* intelligo,' and altered Holofernes' French (misprinted 'Bome boon for
boon' in the original editions) into *'Bone?—bone* for
bene.' But the schoolmaster's meaning is that the
sentence is Priscian (correct Latin), but scratched by
overuse. He would never admit that a positive error
in grammar 'will serve.'

V. i. 45.   *honorificabilitudinitatibus.* Dative (or
ablative) plural of a genuine mediæval Latin word
used by Dante and other writers. It was famous as
the longest of all words. It means something like 'the
state of being capable of honors.'

V. i. 50.   *horn-book.* A rudimentary implement of
education. It consisted in a paper containing the letters of the alphabet, Lord's Prayer, etc., fastened to
a piece of board and protected by a covering of
transparent horn.

V. i. 73.   *circum circa.* This is Theobald's rather
over-ingenious emendation of *'vnum cita'* in the early
editions. Hart proposes *'unciatim,'* inch by inch, and
the late Cambridge editors *nimis cito,* all too quickly.
Furness thinks *unum cita* a meaningless bit of school-
boy slang.

V. i. 82.   *ad dunghill.* This, as Holofernes suspects, is a perversion of *ad unguem,* probably current
in the grammar-schools.

V. i. 88, 89.   *the charge-house on the top of the
mountain.* Charge-house, defined as boarding-school
in the Oxford Dictionary, is not otherwise exemplified.
The mention of the top of the mountain has been sus-
pected of containing some topical reference. Critics
who wish to identify Holofernes with John Florio take

mountain as suggesting Montaigne, whose essays
Florio translated. The date of Florio's Montaigne,
1603, seems sufficient to discredit this theory.

V. i. 128. *the Nine Worthies.* They were variously
listed, the most common enumeration being:—Three
pagans (Hector, Alexander, and Cæsar); three Jews
(Joshua, David, and Judas Maccabæus); and three
Christians (King Arthur, Charlemagne, and Godfrey
of Bouillon). Hercules and Pompey seem to have
been first included by Shakespeare.

V. i. 145. *Hercules in minority.* The myth related
that the infant Hercules' first exploit was to strangle
two serpents which Juno had sent to destroy him.
Hart quotes a line from Golding's Ovid (*Metamorpho-
ses* ix. 79, 80), which may have stuck in the poet's
memory: 'It is my Cradle game To vanquish Snakes.'

V. ii. 13. *You'll ne'er be friends with him: a' kill'd
your sister.* M. Abel Lefranc (*Sous le Masque de
'William Shakespeare,'* 1919, ii. p. 73-80) identifies
this sister of Katharine with Hélène de Tournon, an
attendant of Marguerite de Valois, Queen of Navarre,
who actually died of love in 1577. But the incident
is so similar to Viola's famous story of her sister in
Twelfth Night that it seems more likely to have come
from something in the personal experience of the poet
than from anything in the source material of *Love's
Labour's Lost.*

V. ii. 26. *I weigh not you.* A pun, as the next
line shows, on two idioms: (1) 'I do not equal you in
weight,' and (2) 'I don't care about you.'

V. ii. 40. *Much in the letters, nothing in the praise.*
Furness explains 'The resemblance was great in the
dark colour of the letters, but not at all in the sub-
stance of the praise.'

V. ii. 42. *Fair as a text B in a copy-book.* A large
ornamental capital in the old 'Gothic' hand: a 'black-
letter.'

V. ii. 43. *'Ware pencils, ho!* If we come to painting each other's portraits, take care.

V. ii. 44. *red dominical.* The red letter used in old almanacs to mark the Sundays of the year. The mediæval name for Sunday was 'dies dominica.'

V. ii. 51. *A huge translation of hypocrisy.* Katharine affects to think Dumaine's verses imitated from foreign rimers.

V. ii. 61. *in by the week.* Permanently caught.

V. ii. 65. *hests.* The only argument for this word (which editors unanimously admit to be decisive) is the requirement of a rime for 'jests' in the next line. The First Quarto and First Folio read 'deuice,' for which the Second Folio substituted 'behests.' So in line 74 wantonness is a Second Folio emendation of 'wantons be.'

V. ii. 67. *So perttaunt-like would I o'ersway his state.* Not very satisfactorily explained. The numerous conjectural emendations—pedant-like, portent-like, pendant-like, planet-like, etc.—are unconvincing. Marshall argues that perttaunt-like may be the term *'pur tant'* (for so much) used in the card game of Post and Pair, quoting a line from John Davies' *Wittes Pilgrimage* (1610?): 'Then to Pur Tant hee's in subjection.' (Cf. Works of John Davies of Hereford, ed. Grosart, vol. ii. p. 38.)

V. ii. 121. *Like Muscovites or Russians.* Russian costumes were not uncommon in English courtly masquerades. Sir Sidney Lee suggests a particular allusion to a visit of Russian nobles to Elizabeth's court in 1583.

V. ii. 243. *What! was your vizard made without a tongue?* Mr. W. J. Lawrence explains (*Times Lit. Suppl.*, June 7, 1923) that Elizabethan masks were kept in place by a tongue held between the wearer's teeth.

V. ii. 248. *'Veal,' quoth the Dutchman.* 'Veal'

may be the Dutchman's pronunciation of 'well,' or the German *viel* (much), or a pun on 'veil' in the sense of mask. The editors' efforts to evolve wit and sense out of this dialogue are all far-fetched. Katharine is evidently punning on Longaville's name in the words 'long' (l. 245) and 'veal.'

V. ii. 250. *Let's part the word.* The recent Cambridge editors explain: 'half the word "calf" is "ca" which are the first two letters of Catharine, and "half" means "wife." '

V. ii. 280. *Qualm, perhaps.* Pronounced 'calm'; hence the pun. The same jest occurs in *2 Henry IV* II. iv. 39-41.

V. ii. 282. *statute-caps.* An act of Parliament in 1571 required all ordinary citizens to wear woollen caps on Sundays and holidays. Hart quotes a still more apposite regulation for the apparel of London apprentices (in 1582), forbidding them at any time to wear within the city any head covering except a woollen cap. The object was to encourage the wool trade. It is worth noting that Shakespeare's uncle incurred a fine in 1583 for refusing to wear a cloth cap on Sundays and holidays.

V. ii. 339. *Till this man show'd thee.* Theobald first read 'man' for the 'madman' of the early editions, which spoils the scansion of the line and certainly does not improve the sense. A plausible explanation of the intrusion of the superfluous 'mad—' is that the compositor's eye caught the first syllable of 'madam' in the next line.

V. ii. 406. *like a blind harper's song.* Harping was proverbially the resource of the blind.

V. ii. 420. *'Lord have mercy on us.'* The words put up on plague-stricken houses.

V. ii. 424. *the Lord's tokens.* Spots on the body, marking the plague. Berowne jestingly so calls the lords' tokens, i.e. the gifts of his three associates to the ladies who are wearing them. There is perhaps in these plague mentions a suggestion of the great London plague of 1592-1593, but Mr. Charlton argues that such jesting would not be natural while the actual plague was raging.

V. ii. 491. *You cannot beg us.* This slangy way of saying, 'We are no idiots,' seems to have arisen from the practice of suing for the guardianship of wealthy incompetents.

V. ii. 517, 518. *Where zeal strives to content, and the contents Dies in the zeal of that which it presents.* Where the unintelligent zeal of the actors strives to content the audience, and the gist (contents) of the entertainment is destroyed by this very zeal in performance.

V. ii. 545. *Abate throw at novum.* Alluding to a game called novem quinque, in which the two principal throws were nine and five. The Cambridge editors explain the words as 'referring to the presentation of nine worthies by five players.'

V. ii. 549. *With libbard's head on knee.* Theobald explained this by quoting Cotgrave's definition of the French word *masquine:* 'The representation of a lion's head, etc., upon the elbow or knee of some old-fashioned garments.'

V. ii. 566. *it stands too right.* The point seems to be that Alexander's head sat crookedly on his shoulders. Shakespeare can have got this fact from North's Plutarch. Boyet may, however, simply mean that Nathaniel's nose is not aquiline enough for that of a worthy.

V. ii. 576. *You will be scraped out of the painted cloth for this.* That is, you will lose your place as one of the worthies. Painted cloths were a more humble substitute for tapestry in wall-coverings, and the nine worthies were a common subject of their decoration.

V. ii. 577. *your lion, that holds his poll-axe sitting on a close-stool.* Theobald illustrated this Rabelaisian witticism very neatly by quoting the description of Alexander's arms in Gerard Leigh's *Accidence of Armory*, 1591: 'a lion or [of gold color] seiante [sitting] in a chair, holding a battle-axe argent.'

V. ii. 601. *A kissing traitor.* Alluding to the kiss of Judas Iscariot. Berowne gets the hint for this gibe from Dumaine's *clipt* in the line above. Dumaine uses the word in the sense of abbreviated, and Berowne seizes upon another sense, from 'clip,' to embrace.

V. ii. 607. *Judas was hanged on an elder.* An old belief. Sir John Mandeville reported that the tree was still standing.

V. ii. 619. *worn in the cap of a toothdrawer.* The brooch in the toothdrawer's cap appears to have been a distinguishing mark of his costume. Halliwell quoted a passage from the works of John Taylor, the Water-Poet (1630):—'In Queen Elizabeth's days there was a fellow that wore a brooch in his hat like a toothdrawer.' One of the costume sketches made by Inigo Jones for a mask at James I's court represents a toothdrawer wearing a very high hat with a brooch in the left side. (See publications of the (Old) Shakespeare Society, vol. 39, 1848.)

V. ii. 692. *More Ates.* Ate was goddess of discord. She is introduced at the opening of Peele's *Arraignment of Paris* and again in the fourth book of the *Fairy Queen*.

V. ii. 731, 732. *I have seen the day of wrong through the little hole of discretion.* 'To see day at a little hole' was a proverbial saying.

V. ii. 748, 749. *The extreme parts of time extremely forms All causes to the purpose of his speed.* The closing moments of a period force concentration upon the matter in hand, or subordinate everything else to the necessity of making the most of time.

'Forms' is the old northern English plural, frequent in Shakespeare. Cf. 'runs' in line 310.

V. ii. 762. *And by these badges understand the king.* Badges are distinguishing marks. Berowne goes on to explain what they are; namely, the various evidences of the deep sincerity of the wooers' love.

V. ii. 824. *Hence ever then.* The Folio reading. The Quarto has 'Hence herrite then,' which Professor Pollard ingeniously explains as 'Hence hermit then.'

V. ii. 825-830. These six lines evidently come from the earlier version of the play. The expanded version is found in ll. 845-877. See note on IV. iii. 299-304. Mr. Dover Wilson suggests that ll. 878, 879 originally followed 830, and that the whole passage 831-877 was interpolated in the revision, Dumaine being then given in l. 831 the line of Berowne (825) which the poet intended to delete along with Rosaline's original answer (826-830).

V. ii. 844. *The liker you; few taller are so young.* Time in being long is the more like Longaville, who is 'long' both by name and by being tall for his age.

V. ii. 899. *This side is Hiems, Winter; this Ver, the Spring.* The poetical argument between winter and spring was a famous subject of the mediæval *debate*. One version, entitled *Conflictus Hiemis et Veris,* is ascribed to the celebrated Alcuin (*A.D.* 735-804).

APPENDIX A

Sources of the Play

The central idea of *Love's Labour's Lost*—that a
scholarly prince binds himself and his chosen associates to a quasi-monastic scheme of life, which is immediately shattered by the intrusion of amorous senti-
ment[1]—would seem much too obvious to be the original
invention of Shakespeare; yet no earlier work, either
of fiction or of history, has been discovered which can
reasonably be regarded as a source of the play, and
modern scholarship can only repeat, as regards the
main plot, the confession of the first great detector of
Shakespearean sources, Langbaine (1691): 'Loves
Labour Lost (*sic*), a Comedy: the Story of which I
can give no Account of.' Even more, then, than *A
Midsummer-Night's Dream* and *The Tempest*, *Love's
Labour's Lost* stands out as an example of Shakespeare's rare practice of inventing rather than adapt-
ing a dramatic plot.

Like the main plot, the constituent elements which
make up the play owe little, apparently, to Shakespeare's reading. They seem rather to be drawn from
two non-literary sources upon which the play depends
in nearly equal degree. The less conspicuous half of
it—involving the characters of Costard, Jaquenetta,
Dull, Holofernes, and Nathaniel, and the show of
the Nine Worthies—is a heightened study of English
country types, evidently founded upon personal observation. The other half, dealing with the French
lords and ladies, seems based—in so far as it has a
basis outside the poet's imagination—upon the politi-

[1] This idea is evidently a kind of reverse of that in
Tennyson's poem, *The Princess*.

cal talk of London in the period about 1589.[1] In 1880
(Sir) Sidney Lee pointed out three features of this
part of the play which bear an analogy to contemporary history:

(1) The King of Navarre, Berowne, Longaville,
and Dumaine have names which are identical or prac-
tically so with those of four conspicuous leaders in the
French civil war of 1589-1593: Henri IV (Henry of
Navarre); his two generals, Marshal Biron and the
Duke of Longueville; and his great opponent, the
Duke du Maine, or de Mayenne, brother to the Duke
of Guise.[2]

(2) In 1586 Catherine de Medici, Queen-Mother
of France, conducted a diplomatic conference with
Henry of Navarre at St.-Bris, at which the Queen
attempted to influence the course of negotiations by
means of a band of gay and charming ladies in wait-
ing.[3]

[1] Several recent writers see English topical references in
the Princess of France's visit to Navarre. Thus Mr. Arthur
Acheson (*Shakespeare's Lost Years in London*, 1920, p. 119,
165 ff.) conjectures that *Love's Labour's Lost* 'was written
late in 1591, or early in 1592, as a reflection of the
Queen's progress [August, 1591] to Cowdray House, the
home of the Earl of Southampton's maternal grandfather,
Viscount Montague, and that the shooting of deer by the
Princess and her ladies fancifully records phases of the
entertainments arranged for the Queen during her visit.'
Cf. note on IV. i. 112.

[2] Dumaine is prominent in Marlowe's *Massacre at Paris*
as an enemy of Navarre. It is very likely, as Hart and
Charlton diffidently suggest, that Shakespeare confused him
with Marshal d'Aumont, who, though originally anti-Hugue-
not, was one of the first to recognize Navarre after Henri
III's death (1589) and shared with him in the victory at
Ivry (1590). Longueville gained a great victory for the
Huguenots at Senlis in 1589. Lee's further assumption that
Moth is named after La Motte, a French ambassador at
Elizabeth's court in earlier days, lacks probability.

[3] Lefranc would substitute for the meeting at St.-Bris
an earlier meeting of Catherine and Navarre at Nérac in
1580.

(3) In 1582-1583 an official deputation of Muscovites was at Queen Elizabeth's court to treat concerning the marriage of the Czar Ivan to a kinswoman of the English Queen. They made themselves ridiculous and became the butt of a practical joke. (See V. ii. 121 and note.)

The pertinence of these parallels is hardly questionable, but the flippancy and vagueness with which Shakespeare utilizes the historical incidents certainly suggest that his knowledge comes from current talk rather than from definite printed accounts. The dramatist, of course, was not purporting to write contemporary history, as Marlowe was when he produced his *Massacre at Paris*. Doubtless Shakespeare first devised his fiction of Navarre and France at a period when it was possible to weave into it recent names and incidents still too vague in their connotation for English auditors to jar against the playful spirit of the comedy.[1] He seems to have conceived of his Navarre, Berowne, Longaville, and Dumaine as living in some pleasant remote time, and it is entirely possible that the real nucleus of the Navarre-France portion of the story is to be found in some such passage as that of Monstrelet's history,[2] cited by Hunter in 1845, the relevancy of which Lee and nearly all subsequent critics have denied. Monstrelet writes as follows: 'At this same season [*ca.* 1403], Charles king of Navarre came to Paris to wait on the king. He negotiated so successfully with the king and his privy council, that he obtained a gift of the castle of Nemours, with some of its dependent castlewicks, which territory was made

[1] See Appendix B.
[2] Monstrelet, who died in 1453, continued the Chronicles of Froissart from the year 1400. The passage quoted comes near the commencement of his work (bk. i, ch. 17). A number of French editions were available in Shakespeare's time, but there appears to have been no translation into English before that of Thomas Johnes in 1809.

a duchy. He instantly did homage for it, and at the same time surrendered to the king the castle of Cherbourg, the county of Évreux, and all other lordships he possessed within the kingdom of France, renouncing all claim or profit in them to the king and his successors, on consideration that with this duchy of Nemours the king of France engaged to pay him two hundred thousand gold crowns of the coin of the king our lord.' In this rather complicated transaction Shakespeare may have found the suggestion for the still more complex business of the play, in which likewise a deceased King Charles (cf. II. i. 162) of Navarre and a total sum of two hundred thousand crowns (cf. II. i. 128-134) are involved.[1]

The French and English halves of the play are joined together by the characters of Armado and his page Moth, who are neither French nor convincingly English. In these two figures literary precedent is more evident than elsewhere, and it is clearly John Lyly whom Shakespeare is following. Compare the talk of Armado and Moth in II. i with the following scene between a braggart and his page in Lyly's *Endimion*.[2]

'*Sir Tophas*. Epi, loue hath iustled my libertie from the wall, and taken the vpper hand of my reason.
Epiton. Let mee then trippe vp the heeles of your affection, and thrust your goodwill into the gutter.
Sir. To. No, Epi, Loue is a Lorde of misrule, and keepeth Christmas in my corps.
Epi. No doubt there is good cheere: what dishes of delight doth his Lordshippe feast you withal?

---

[1] Professor Lefranc (*Sous le Masque de 'William Shakespeare'*) makes an important addition by showing that discussions concerning Navarre's holdings in the province of Aquitaine were rife between him and the King of France about 1580.
[2] Act V, sc. ii. The date of *Endimion* is probably 1586.

Sir To. First, with a great platter of plum-porridge of pleasure, wherein is stued the mutton of mistrust.

Epi. Excellent loue lappe.

Sir To. Then commeth a Pye of patience, a Henne of honnie, a Goose of gall, a Capon of care, and many other Viandes, some sweete and some sowre; which proueth loue to bee, as it was saide of in olde yeeres, *Dulce venenum.*

Epi. A braue banquet.

Sir To. But, Epi, I praye thee feele on my chinne, some thing prycketh mee. What dost thou feele or see?

Epi. There are three or foure little haires.

Sir To. I pray thee call it my bearde. Howe shall I bee troubled when this younge springe shall growe to a great wood!

Epi. O, sir, your chinne is but a quyller yet, you will be most maiesticall when it is full fledge. But I maruell that you loue *Dipsas,* that old Crone,' etc.

The chief literary influence in *Love's Labour's Lost* is certainly Lyly's, poor though the latter's work seems by contrast. Shakespeare at once differentiates himself from the artificial prose comedy of Lyly by his vindication of common sense against affectation and by his deep interest in sonorous verse effects. It is not unlikely that the play is also related superficially to Marlowe's *Massacre at Paris* (written toward the end of 1589), in which the historical Navarre and Dumaine are both introduced, and which opens with Navarre's marriage to the Princess of France.[1]

[1] Dr. Johnson made the plausible conjecture that Shakespeare's character of Holofernes owes something to the pedantic schoolmaster, Rombus, in Sir Philip Sidney's pastoral play, *The Lady of May,* acted before Queen Elizabeth in 1578.

APPENDIX B

SHAKESPEARE'S ORIGINAL TEXT AND HIS REVISION

The date of composition of Shakespeare's original (lost) version of *Love's Labour's Lost* and its relation to the text of 1598, corrected and augmented for performance at court, have been the subject of long discussion, to which daring contributions have been made within the last half-dozen years. The conjectured dates of original composition range, according to Dr. Furness' table, from 1588 or earlier till after 1596. Metrical evidence, persisting even in the augmented text, supports the assumption of Furnivall, Dowden, and Sir Sidney Lee that *Love's Labour's Lost* is the earliest of all Shakespeare's plays. Hart (Arden ed., x-xvii) finds other internal evidence pointing 'to 1590 for the date of the earliest form of the play.' Such till recently has been the generally accepted opinion.

In the *Modern Language Review* (July, October, 1918) Mr. H. B. Charlton published a monograph on 'The Date of *Love's Labour's Lost*,' in which he argues for the latter part of 1592 as the time of first composition and assumes only a slight revision immediately previous to the performance of 1597-8. Subsequent writers have apparently inclined to accept Mr. Charlton's rather iconoclastic conclusions. Professor J. Q. Adams[1] agrees that '1592 is the earliest date that can possibly be assigned to the play,' and conjectures that it was composed during the inhibition of acting from June till December of that year. The recent Cambridge editors (1923) go farther and, joining Mr.

[1] *Life of Shakespeare*, 1923, p. 142 f. Compare Professor O. F. Emerson in an article on 'Shakespeare's Sonneteering,' *Studies in Philology*, April, 1923, p. 122.

Charlton's deductions to some fancied evidences in the play of hostility to Sir Walter Raleigh and his associates, arrive at 1593 for the year of writing: 'We give it as our belief, and no more, that *Love's Labour's Lost* was written in 1593 for a private performance in the house of some grandee who had opposed Raleigh and Raleigh's "men"—possibly the Earl of Southampton's.'

I venture to suggest briefly some reasons for thinking that the probability of an early version of *Love's Labour's Lost,* written not later than 1590 and standing very near the beginning of Shakespeare's dramatic work, remains unimpaired.[1] Mr. Charlton agrees that Shakespeare's use of topical names (Navarre, Berowne, Longaville, Dumaine) is a concession to English interest in contemporary events in France. This interest, he maintains, really began with the sending of an expeditionary force to the aid of Henry of Navarre in July, 1591, while 'the summer and autumn of 1592 marked the highest level of English public interest in the French wars.'[2] It seems clear, on the other hand, that if Shakespeare gave his sentimental students these topical names out of consideration for public interest in their namesakes, he could only have done so before the public, or he himself, had yet

[1] I do not deal with the special allusions which Mr. Charlton finds in individual passages of the play to books and events of the period 1590-1592. In most cases the dates implied do not seem to me decisive, and Mr. Charlton's unsupported hypothesis that practically everything in the play was in it from the beginning removes the matter from the field of argument.

[2] Dr. Furnivall refers to Stow's statement that in September, 1589, 'the citizens of London furnished a thousand men to be sent over into France, to the aiding of Henry, late King of Navarre, then challenging the crown of France.' Mr. Charlton rather perversely, as it seems to me, refuses to believe that there can have been sufficient public interest at this date.

acquired any clear notion of the character and achieve-
ments of the latter. To call the King of Navarre
Ferdinand rather than Henry and ignore his preten-
sions to the French crown, to say nothing (virtually)
of the military fame of the four gentlemen and asso-
ciate Dumaine in friendship with the rest, or alter-
natively, to confuse Dumaine with d'Aumont,[1] would
have affronted common intelligence if attempted very
long after the death of Henri III (August 2, 1589)
had brought them all upon the centre of the political
stage. I take it that the period between Henri III's
assassination and the battle of Ivry (March 14, 1590)
was the latest at which an English dramatist could
have thought of thus irrelevantly employing the names
of the leading French generals for the heroes of a
comedy of love and the simple life.

Mr. Charlton's assumption that the revision of the
play was slight is contradicted by the large amount of
discrepancy between mature and immature work, and
also by the curious and cumbrous structure of the
existing text, in which the first three acts together are
only half the length of the last two and not as long as
the colossal second scene of Act V.

The first three acts doubtless represent the scale
upon which the comedy was originally written. The
earliest critic who attempted to distinguish closely
between the two texts (of *ca.* 1590 and *ca.* 1597) appears to have been Spedding, whose apportionment,
made in 1839, is quoted by Dr. Furnivall.[2] In a
paper on 'The Original Version of *Love's Labour's
Lost*' (1918) Professor H. D. Gray has attempted
with interesting results to discover the scope of the
original play, basing his arguments upon evidences
of organic unity and 'youthful love of symmetry,' as

---

[1] See Appendix A, p. 128, note 2.
[2] Facsimile of 1598 Quarto, pp. viii, ix; Leopold Shak-
spere, p. xxiii.

well as upon style. In the recent Cambridge edition Mr. Dover Wilson has made a similar attempt,[1] independently and by means of totally different criteria— chiefly the bibliographical phenomena of the Quarto and Folio texts. The various results are of course contradictory in many details, but the investigators all agree in assigning a large preponderance of the first three acts to the original version and the larger part of the last two to the revision.

[1] The results are summarized on p. 116, of the Cambridge edition.

APPENDIX C

The History of the Play

The known history of *Love's Labour's Lost* begins with the evidence found on the title-page of the earliest edition,[1] the Quarto of 1598. This reads: 'A Pleasant Conceited Comedie Called, Loues labors lost. As it vvas presented before her Highnes this last Christmas. Newly corrected and augmented By W. Shakespere.' Her Highness was Queen Elizabeth and the Christmas performance alluded to probably took place during the season of December, 1597-January, 1598.[2] The statement that the play had been newly corrected and augmented is substantiated beyond all question by the text itself, particularly in the fourth and fifth acts.[3]

Love's Labour's Lost is the earliest of Shakespeare's plays concerning which we have notice of a special performance at court and probably also the earliest to name Shakespeare as author on the printed title-page. It is mentioned in Meres' *Palladis Tamia* (1598),

[1] Mr. Pollard has argued that this Quarto was probably preceded by a piratical earlier edition of which no trace remains. The evidence is purely bibliographical and circumstantial, but carries weight.

[2] The Elizabethan year began with March 25. Hence if the Quarto was printed between January 1 and March 24, 'this last Christmas' would be Christmas, 1598, by our reckoning. Halliwell-Phillipps (Furness, p. 336) suggested a connection of the performance of the play with a recorded payment in December, 1597, 'for altering and making readie of soundrie chambers at Whitehall against Christmas, and for the plaies, and for making readie in the hall for her Maiestie.' Shakespeare's company acted at court on December 26 of both years, 1597 and 1598, and also on the following January 1 (1598 and 1599).

[3] See notes on IV. iii. 299-304 and V. ii. 825-830.

third in the list of six comedies ascribed to the poet,
and again in the same year in Robert Tofte's *Alba,*
where the allusion is casual and more complimentary
to the actors than to the dramatist:

'Loues Labor Lost, I once did see a Play
    Ycleped so, so called to my paine,
Which I to heare to my small Ioy did stay,
    Giuing attendance on my froward Dame,
        My misgiuing minde presaging to me Ill,
        Yet was I drawne to see it gainst my Will.

'This Play no Play, but Plague was vnto me,
    For there I lost the Loue I liked most:
And what to others seemde a Iest to be,
    I that in earnest found vnto my cost:
        To euery one (saue me) twas Comicall,
        Whilst Tragick like to me it did befall.

'Each Actor plaid in cunning wise his part,
    But chiefly Those entrapt in Cupids snare:
Yet all was fained, twas not from the hart,
    They seemde to grieue, but yet they felt no care:
        Twas I that Griefe (indeed) did beare in brest,
        The others did but make a show in Iest.'

The sonnets of Berowne (IV. ii. 110-123) and
Longaville (IV. iii. 60-73) and Dumaine's 'ode' (IV.
iii. 101-120) were reprinted by William Jaggard in
1599 in the pirated volume called *The Passionate Pil-
grim,* and Dumaine's poem was also included in the
anthology, *England's Helicon,* in 1600. Later William Drummond of Hawthornden lists the comedy as
one of the 'Bookes red be me, *anno* 1606,' when Drummond was staying in London. Property rights in the
published play are affirmed when, on January 22,
1606/7, Burby, the publisher of the 1598 Quarto
(who seems not to have entered it himself), transferred

Love's Labour's Lost, along with *Romeo and Juliet* and *The Taming of a Shrew* to Nicholas Linge. Less than a year later Linge surrendered all three plays (November 19, 1607) to John Smethwick, who was later one of the partners in the Folio Shakespeare.

Though probably never notably popular, *Love's Labour's Lost* showed unusual staying powers during the Shakespearean era. First produced at the opening of the poet's career, it was rewritten, as we have seen, in 1597-8 for the particular amusement of Queen Elizabeth. A little over a year after her death it was again selected for court performance in order to divert her successor, Anne of Denmark (Queen of James I), as is witnessed by the following very interesting letter from Sir Walter Cope to Viscount Cranborne (i.e. Sir Robert Cecil, later Lord Salisbury):

'Sir,—I haue sent and bene all thys morning huntyng for players Juglers & Such kinde of Creaturs, but fynde them harde to fynde; wherefore leauing notes for them to seek me, Burbage ys come, and sayes there is no new playe that the quene hath not seene, but they haue reuyued an olde one, cawled *Loves Labore Lost,* which for wytt & mirthe he sayes will please her exceedingly. And thys ys appointed to be playd to morrowe night at my Lord of Sowthamptons, unless yow send a wrytt to remove the corpus *cum causa* to your howse in Strande. Burbage ys my messenger ready attending your pleasure.' This is dated '1604,' and the performance referred to is fixed by Mr. Chambers as between January 8 and January 15, 1604/5.[1] The audit office accounts for 1604-5 record the acting 'By his Majesty's players' of 'A play of Loues Labours Lost' between New Year's Day and Twelfth Day (January 6).

A certain degree of continued popularity is indicated by the publication of another Quarto edition of

[1] *Elizabethan Stage,* iv. 139 f.

Love's Labour's Lost in 1631, during the period, that is, between the appearance of the first and second Folio editions of Shakespeare, when relatively few of his plays were being called for in separate form. The statement on the title-page of this Quarto, 'As it was acted by his Majesty's Servants at the Blackfriars and the Globe,' if correct, proves that revivals must have occurred after 1608-9, when Shakespeare's company first began to use the Blackfriars' Theatre.

Later the play fell into total obscurity for over a century. No performances or adaptations are known during the period of the Restoration or the first half of the eighteenth century. Dryden in 1672[1] groups *Love's Labour's Lost* with *The Winter's Tale* and *Measure for Measure* as examples of the worst of Shakespeare's plays, 'which were either grounded on impossibilities, or at least so meanly written, that the comedy neither caused your mirth, nor the serious part your concernment.' Jeremy Collier (1699) says briefly of it that 'the poet plays the fool egregiously, for the whole play is a very silly one'; and Gildon (1710) brands it as 'one of the worst of Shakespear's Plays, nay, I think I may say, the very worst.'

When *As You Like It* was revived in 1740, the cuckoo song from the close of *Love's Labour's Lost* was interpolated into the acting version of the other play, where it long continued to be used.[2] This would seem to be the only part of *Love's Labour's Lost* that ever appeared on the eighteenth-century stage. The first known adaptation of our play was printed in 1762 with the title: 'The Students. A Comedy Altered from Shakespeare's Love's Labours Lost, and Adapted to the Stage.' Though equipped with elaborate pro-

---

[1] *The Conquest of Granada, Pt. II.* Defence of the Epilogue.

[2] Cf. Furness, p. 316, note on line 976. Both the cuckoo song and the other song of winter were printed in 1671 in an anthology called *The New Academy of Compliments.*

logue and epilogue in heroic couplets, there is no evidence that this work ever reached the stage for which
it had been 'adapted.' Only about 800 lines of the
original play are retained;[1] the characters of Holofernes and Nathaniel are omitted entirely, and the
mask of Muscovites and show of Nine Worthies are
replaced by a 'comic dance' in dumb-show. The al-
terations of Shakespeare's main plot are rather re-
markable. Berowne puts on a coat intended for
Costard, and having thus easily rendered himself
irrecognizable, carries messages between the lords and
ladies. In this way he secures information enough
about the real sentiments of them all to dominate the
situation and force an immediate happy ending instead of the year's postponement proposed by the
Princess. His closing words express the author's high
sense of his improvement upon the original:

> 'Our wooing now doth end like an old play;
> Jack hath his Jill; these ladies' courtesie
> Hath nobly made our sport a Comedy.'

Another apparently unacted revision of *Love's Labour's Lost,* likewise anonymous, is preserved in a
single copy at the British Museum. It dates from
about the year 1800. This version also eliminates
Holofernes and Nathaniel and concludes with the
ladies' consent to immediate matrimony, brought about
in a manner quite different from that employed in
The Students. The characters of Costard and Jaquenetta (Jaquelina) are much romanticized, and they too
are made happy at the end. Armado is presented as
a demi-villain, and eavesdropping is employed even
more copiously than in the original play.

On September 30, 1839, the first recorded performance of *Love's Labour's Lost* since Shakespearean

---

[1] As counted by F. Schult, *Bühnenbearbeitungen von
Shakespeares "Love's Labour's Lost,"* 1910.

times was given at Covent Garden. Madame Vestris played Rosaline; Harley, Armado; and Anderson, Berowne. The piece was performed nine times and three slightly differing versions of the acting text were published. In 1857 Samuel Phelps presented the play at the Sadler's Wells Theatre, Phelps himself taking the part of Armado. In 1885 and again in 1907 it was produced at the Memorial Theatre, Stratford-on-Avon, as the Shakespeare Birthday play (April 23), Mr. F. R. Benson playing Berowne on the latter occasion. The English Drama Society gave it in Bloomsbury Hall, April 24, 1906. Other productions are recorded by the companies of Charles Fry, Ben Greet, and Florence Glossop-Harris. An acting version, 'adapted by Elsie Fogerty for Girls' Schools,' was published in 1912. Recently, under the management of Miss Lillian Baylis, *Love's Labour's Lost* has appeared frequently in the repertory of the Royal Victoria Hall ('Old Vic.') in London; e.g. in the spring of 1918 and during the season that began September 22, 1923. The most recent production was that given by the Oxford University Dramatic Society in Wadham College garden, June 21, 1924. The enthusiastic tone of the critics of these late performances[1] shows that the play is now gaining in the esteem of audiences as during the past generation it has gained in the favor of critics and general readers.

The most important American productions of *Love's Labour's Lost* were those arranged by Augustin Daly in New York, in 1874 and again in 1891. The German Shakespeare scholar, Rudolph Genée, brought out in 1887 a considerably altered version in three acts for the German stage. In recent times this has usually been supplanted by translations which adhere more closely to the original.

[1] See reviews, for example, in the *Manchester Guardian,* September 28, 1923, and June 27, 1924.

APPENDIX D

The Text of the Present Edition

The text of the present volume is based, by permission of the Oxford University Press, upon that of the Oxford Shakespeare, edited by the late W. J. Craig, and the line-numbering of that edition, employed in Onions' *Shakespeare Glossary* and other works of reference, has been retained. Craig's text has been carefully collated with the two primary authorities, the 1598 Quarto and the text of *Love's Labour's Lost* in the Folio of 1623, and the following changes have been made:

1. The stage directions of the two original editions have been restored. They vary only in a few unimportant details. Necessary words and directions, omitted by both Quarto and Folio, are supplied within square brackets.

2. Punctuation and spelling have been normalized to accord with modern English practice; e.g. Anthony, godlike, malcontents, nickname, villainy (instead of Antony, god-like, malecontents, nick-name, villany). Legitimate Shakespearean words have been retained; e.g. ballet, murtherer, strooken, vizard (instead of ballad, murderer, strucken, visor).

3. The following changes of text have been introduced, nearly always in conformity with Quarto and Folio authority (indicated by Q and F respectively). Where the two differ, the Quarto has usually been preferred. Changes of punctuation are noted only when they materially affect the sense. The readings of the present edition precede the colon, while Craig's readings follow it:

I. i. 104	any QF: an
	106	shows QF: mirth
	114	what I have sworn QF: to what I swore
	165	who QF: whom
	192	low QF: long (misprint?)
	260	with—but: with but
	270	an't shall QF: an 't
288, 289, 290	damsel Q: damosel F
ii. 55	here is Q: here's F
		ye'll Q: you'll F
	135	suffer him to Q: let him F
	187	cause QF: clause (misprint?)
II. i. 25	to's seemeth QF: to us seem'th
	39	Longaville QF: Lord Longaville
	42	Falconbridge solemnized, QF: Falconbridge, solemnized
	88	unpeopled F: unpeeled Q
	127	will I QF: I will (misprint?)
217, 219, 220, 222	{ Kath. Q: Mar. F (See note)
	226	lies,: lies,—
	227	eyes,—: eyes,
	254	Kath.: Ros.
	255	Ros.: Mar.
III. i. 27	note? men: note me (note men QF)
	61	The Q: Thy F
	135	on QF: upon (misprint?)
	154	ribbon QF: riband
	199	What QF: What I
	214	groan QF: and groan
IV. i. 74	Who QF: Whom
	103	Thou fellow QF: Thou, fellow
	125	I may QF: may I
	147	fit. QF: fit,
ii. 4	the Q: a F
	25	in QF: of (misprint?)
	35	tell me Q: tell F
	85	pers-on? And QF: pers-on. An
	89	Of piercing QF: Piercing
iii. 22	Ay QF: Ah
	41	dost thou QF: thou dost
	86	not, QF: but
	106	can QF: 'gan
	146	Faith QF: A faith
	176	by . . . to QF: to . . . by

255 school QF: scowl
345 Make QF: Makes

V. i. 28 ne QF: anne
30 bene QF: bone
31 Bon, bon, fort bon: Bone? bone, for bene (See note)
106 courtesy (QF curtesie): curtsy
131 assistants QF: assistance, at
165 play on QF: play (misprint?)
ii. 11 year Q: years F
43 ho!: how? QF
46 Prin. . . . and I QF: Kath. . . . and
47 But, Katharine QF: Prin. But
139 mockery Q: mocking F
209 requests QF: request'st
210 vouchsafe but F: but vouchsafe (Q do but vouchsafe)
243, 247 vizard QF: visor
272 vizards QF: visors
274 They QF: O! they
310 runs o'er QF: run over
361 pastimes QF: pastime (misprint?)
374 Gentle QF: Fair gentle
386 vizards QF: visors
387, 408, 405 vizard QF: visor
390 were Q: are F
393 sound QF: swound
492 nine?: nine.
506 Pompey QF: Pompion
518 Dies . . . that QF: Die . . . those
527 A' . . . God his Q: He . . . God's F
528 That is Q: That's F
590 canus QF: canis
641 Hector's Q: Hector F
730 mine QF: my
745 humble QF: nimble
746 too Q: so F
748 parts QF: part
771 straying QF: stray
776 misbecom'd QF: misbecome
806 the Q: their F
840 ye QF: you
873 then QF: them
879 an QF: a
893 year Q: years F

APPENDIX E

Walter Pater: Essay on *Love's Labour's Lost* in *Appreciations* (1889), pp. 167-175. (Written in 1878.)

S. L. Lee: 'A New Study of *Love's Labour's Lost.*' *Gentleman's Magazine,* Oct., 1880, vol. 249, pp. 447-458.

Andrew Lang: 'The Comedies of Shakespeare, with Illustrations by E. A. Abbey and Comment by Andrew Lang.' X *Love's Labour's Lost.* *Harper's Magazine,* May, 1893, pp. 900-913.

J. M. Robertson: *Shakespeare and Chapman.* London, 1917, pp. 107-120. (A superior example of 'heretical' criticism. Holofernes is explained as a satire on Chapman.)

H. D. Gray: *The Original Version of 'Love's Labour's Lost,' with a Conjecture as to 'Love's Labour's Won.'* Stanford University Publications, 1918. (Well-informed but over-imaginative.)

H. B. Charlton: *The Date of 'Love's Labour's Lost.'* *Modern Language Review,* July, October, 1918, vol. xiii, pp. 257-266, 387-400. (See discussion, Appendix B, p. 132 ff.)

Abel Lefranc: *Sous le Masque de 'William Shakespeare.'* Paris, 1919. Chap. vii, vol. ii, pp. 17-103. (The book argues that William Stanley, Earl of Derby, wrote Shakespeare. The chapter cited contains interesting data illustrative of *Love's Labour's Lost.*)

Austin K. Gray: *The Secret of 'Love's Labour's Lost.'* Publ. Mod. Lang. Assoc., September, 1924, vol. xxxix, pp. 581-611. (An attempt to explain the play in the light of Lord Southampton's nugatory betrothal to Elizabeth Vere, 1591.)

The Furness Variorum edition of *Love's Labour's Lost,* Philadelphia, 1904, is excellent even beyond the average of its series. That in the Arden series, edited by H. C. Hart, 1906 (2d ed., 1913), contains much valuable illustrative material (the critical conclusions in the Introduction are often exceptionable). The edition of Sir A. Quiller-Couch and Mr. J. Dover Wilson for the Cambridge University Press (1923) exploits the modern methods of bibliographical annotation, often with over-imaginative results.

INDEX OF WORDS GLOSSED

(Figures in full-faced type refer to page-numbers)